TRIATHLON
THE GO FASTER GUIDE

mark barfield

TRIATHLON
THE GO FASTER GUIDE
how to make yourself a quicker triathlete

BLOOMSBURY
LONDON · NEW DELHI · NEW YORK · SYDNEY

Note
While every effort has been made to ensure that the content of this book is as technically accurate and as sound as possible, neither the author nor the publishers can accept responsibility for any injury or loss sustained as a result of the use of this material.

Published by Bloomsbury Publishing Plc
50 Bedford Square
London WC1B 3DP
www.bloomsbury.com

First edition 2013

ISBN (print): 978-1-4088-3227-1

Acknowledgements
Cover photographs © Getty Images
Inside photographs: pp. 2, 9, 18, 21, 25, 33, 69, 91, 113, 121, 123, 137, 141, 143, 149 © Shutterstock; pp. 84–85, 16, 116, 118 © Maxisport/Shutterstock.com; pp. 28–29 © Mark Herreid/Shutterstock.com; p. 35 © Jeffrey Ong Guo Xiong/Shutterstock.com; pp. 6, 40–41, 92 © Alberto Loyo/Shutterstock.com; p. 45 © Iurii Osadchi/Shutterstock.com; p. 53 © Sergei Bachlakov/Shutterstock.com; pp. 54, 105 © Rihardzz/Shutterstock.com; pp. 76–77 © Martin Good/Shutterstock.com; p. 79 © Chris Curtis/ Shutterstock.com; p. 95 © Richard Thornton/Shutterstock.com; pp. 98, 117, 119, 131 © Alain Lauga/Shutterstock.com; pp. 114–115 © ema/Shutterstock.com; p. 120 © blojfo/Shutterstock.com; p. 138 © Efecreata Photography/Shutterstock.com; pp. 146–147 © Valeria73/Shutterstock.com; p. 124 © ARZTSAMUI/Shutterstock.com; pp. 13, 14, 22–23, 60, 72, 102, 142 © Press Association; pp. 38–39, 46–47, 50, 62, 80, 86, 87, 108, 134, 145 © Getty Images.
Illustrations by David Gardner (pp. 30, 68, 89) and Tom Croft (p.104)
Commissioned by Charlotte Croft

This book is produced using paper that is made from wood grown in managed, sustainable forests. It is natural, renewable and recyclable. The logging and manufacturing processes conform to the environmental regulations of the country of origin.

Typeset in URW Grotesk by seagulls.net

Printed and bound in India by Replika Press Pvt Ltd

10 9 8 7 6 5 4 3 2 1

CONTENTS

INTRODUCTION

AIMS AND OBJECTIVES

Triathlon is one of Europe's fastest-growing sports. There are more events, more clubs and more opportunities to compete and improve than ever before. This book is designed to help you make the most of these opportunities, and has been written with people of all levels of experience – from seasoned triathletes to complete novices – in mind. This may seem like a bold claim, but with some simple structure and improved techniques you can create a plan that will help you become a faster, more effective athlete. The basics of this approach can be used for triathlon, *aquathlon* and *duathlon* and will be applicable regardless of your sporting background.

There are no magic secrets in this book, and hard work, good equipment and an appropriate diet will always be necessary, but work must be properly directed, and this book will help you to use your time wisely and achieve your best by using your efforts effectively. While it is certainly true that spending money on equipment won't necessarily make you faster, it is certainly the case that well chosen, well maintained and appropriately prepared equipment will ensure that you get the most out of your hard-earned *fitness*. There are already many comprehensive books on sports nutrition available; my aim is to help you get the basics right in a structure that works for you and is appropriate to your lifestyle, training and racing style.

Triathlon is a sport that offers a huge amount of enjoyment and physical reward, and this book will help you get even more from it by working hard and in the right way.

HOW TO USE THE BOOK

Ultimately, my approach is to help you to help yourself, as people are so diverse that one size really can't fit all. Good coaching is irreplaceable and in many cases this book will be greatly enhanced by seeking out a good coach to help you improve your technique and your tactical and technical awareness of the sport.

I will show you how to apply some structure to your training, how to apply the right kind of training load at the right time and how to plan all of this in a real working situation that is realistic and can be sustained alongside all the other responsibilities in your day-to-day life. The phrase 'train smart' is often used but is seldom understood or properly applied, with the result that many people train too much, frequently without focus or structure. For many people one of the attractions of triathlon is that it embraces large volumes of training in diverse activities – an important fix for the activity junky. You don't necessarily have to turn your back on this completely but there is a balance to be achieved with quality sessions, quality structure and adequate rest. Activity for the sake of activity is pointless and can be detrimental to your training.

I will help you construct your own programme and ask you some key questions that will help to identify if you are training hard enough and in the right way. By working through each section you will end up with plans for each of the disciplines (swimming, cycling and running). You will also have an outline of how to fuel this training and how to develop your own nutritional strategy for events. Towards the end of the book you may start to put all of this together into a cohesive and balanced plan that will focus on your target events. The book will also aid you in identifying a plan that will help you build to faster long-term goals and a better racing future.

A well-designed plan will help you get faster and achieve your goals. This book will give you the information you need to do this. At the back of the book you will find a glossary of useful terms. Terms that appear in this glossary are *italicised* the first time they are used in the book.

PLANNING PRINCIPLES

Assess current position

In order to gauge progress, set goals and break training down into manageable pieces it is essential that you know your position now and at appropriate points during the process. The way to do this is to test your parameters across all three disciplines. The book will work you through this process, and as you develop your training programme you will build in tests at appropriate points to ensure you are improving at the right pace. It is very important that you record your testing data in enough detail that the data is easy to replicate, compare and develop from. This means noting the circumstances around each test including details of work and life commitments in the surrounding days. This will help you understand and minimise the ways in which outside factors affect your results. It is essential that you are honest with yourself about your position at any given time, and you will need to establish what your weaknesses are as well as working on your strengths. People often fall into the trap of training harder in the disciplines they find easier, meaning that their strengths get stronger and their weaknesses remain just that. Achieving this level of honesty with yourself can be very difficult, but you really do need to address your weaknesses in order to become a rounded athlete. Broadly speaking if you were evenly talented across all three disciplines you would look for a programme with an even number of sessions per discipline, with additional time devoted to *transition* training (see Chapter 5). This would not necessarily reflect the number of hours devoted to each discipline as, by their nature, you would spend more time cycling for instance than you would swimming, even if the number of sessions remained the same. If you are weaker at one discipline, you should increase the number of sessions in this discipline while reducing the number of sessions in your stronger disciplines. Technique training will have an impact as well but this will be looked at in Chapters 2, 3 and 4, which deal with the disciplines individually.

PLANNING EXAMPLES

In the appendix at the end of the book are four template planning forms that will help you structure your training. You can photocopy these or download them from www.bloomsbury.com/uk/triathlon-the-go-faster-guide-9781408832271. Each is outlined below with an example plan.

Our first planning form is designed to enable you to work out what time you have to fit in training with the rest of your life commitments. This is really important to ensure you identify the opportunities that you have to train as well as ensuring that you have sufficient time for work, family, rest and other activities.

This example shows an outline of a typical week. There is plenty of free time in it but the training sessions are clearly identified. Of course, with different working life patterns your plan may not be this simple but the principle remains the same: set clearly defined training times during the day and week.

PLANNING FORM EXAMPLE – FITTING IN YOUR WEEKLY TRAINING

	Monday	Tuesday	Wednesday
05.00 a.m.	sleep	sleep	sleep
05.30	sleep	sleep	sleep
06.00		sleep	sleep
06.30	swim	sleep	sleep
07.00	swim		
07.30			
08.00	work	work	work
08.30	work	work	work
09.00	work	work	work
09.30	work	work	work
10.00	work	work	work
10.30	work	work	work
11.00	work	work	work
11.30	work	work	work
Noon	run		run
12.30 p.m.	work	work	work
1.00	work	work	work
1.30	work	work	work
2.00	work	work	work
2.30	work	work	work
3.00	work	work	work
3.30	work	work	work
4.00	work	work	work
4.30	work	work	work
5.00	work	work	work
5.30			
6.00			
6.30			
7.00	s&c*	spinning	swim
7.30		spinning	swim
8.00		s&c	swim
8.30			
9.00			
9.30			
10.00			

* strength and conditioning

Thursday	Friday	Saturday	Sunday
sleep	sleep	sleep	sleep
sleep	sleep	sleep	sleep
	sleep	sleep	sleep
sleep	sleep	sleep	sleep
swim		sleep	sleep
		sleep	sleep
work	work		
work	work		
work	work		
work	work	**run**	**bike**
work	work	**run**	**bike**
work	work	**run**	**bike**
work	work	**run**	**bike**
work	work		**bike**
	run		
work	work		
work	work		
work	work		
work	work		
work			
work	**bike**		
work	**bike**		
work	**bike**		
work	**bike**		
work			
run	pub		
run	pub		
s&c	pub		
	pub		

The second planner provides a long-term view of where you are headed. You can use this for number of sessions in each discipline or to record your goals.

This is quite a superficial example but it shows that the programme builds from a low base and alters focus on the disciplines as it progresses. There are also a number of easy weeks in it and it tapers towards the end, as you approach the event.

PLANNING FORM EXAMPLE – LONG-TERM AND CROSS-DISCIPLINE			
Week	Swim	Bike	Run
1	2 sessions	2 sessions	3 sessions
2	2 sessions	2 sessions	3 sessions
3	2 sessions	2 sessions	3 sessions
4	2 sessions	2 sessions	3 sessions
5	3 sessions	2 sessions	3 sessions
6	3 sessions	2 sessions	3 sessions
7	3 sessions	2 sessions	3 sessions
8	3 sessions	2 sessions	3 sessions
9	4 sessions	3 sessions	3 sessions
10	4 sessions	3 sessions	3 sessions
11	4 sessions	3 sessions	3 sessions
12	4 sessions	3 sessions	3 sessions
13	2 sessions	2 sessions	2 sessions
14	4 sessions	4 sessions	3 sessions
15	4 sessions	4 sessions	3 sessions
16	4 sessions	4 sessions	3 sessions
17	4 sessions	4 sessions	3 sessions
18	4 sessions	3 sessions	4 sessions
19	4 sessions	3 sessions	4 sessions
20	4 sessions	3 sessions	4 sessions
21	4 sessions	3 sessions	4 sessions
22	2 sessions	2 sessions	2 sessions
23	4 sessions	4 sessions	4 sessions
24	4 sessions	4 sessions	4 sessions
25	3 sessions	3 sessions	3 sessions
26	2 sessions	2 sessions	2 sessions

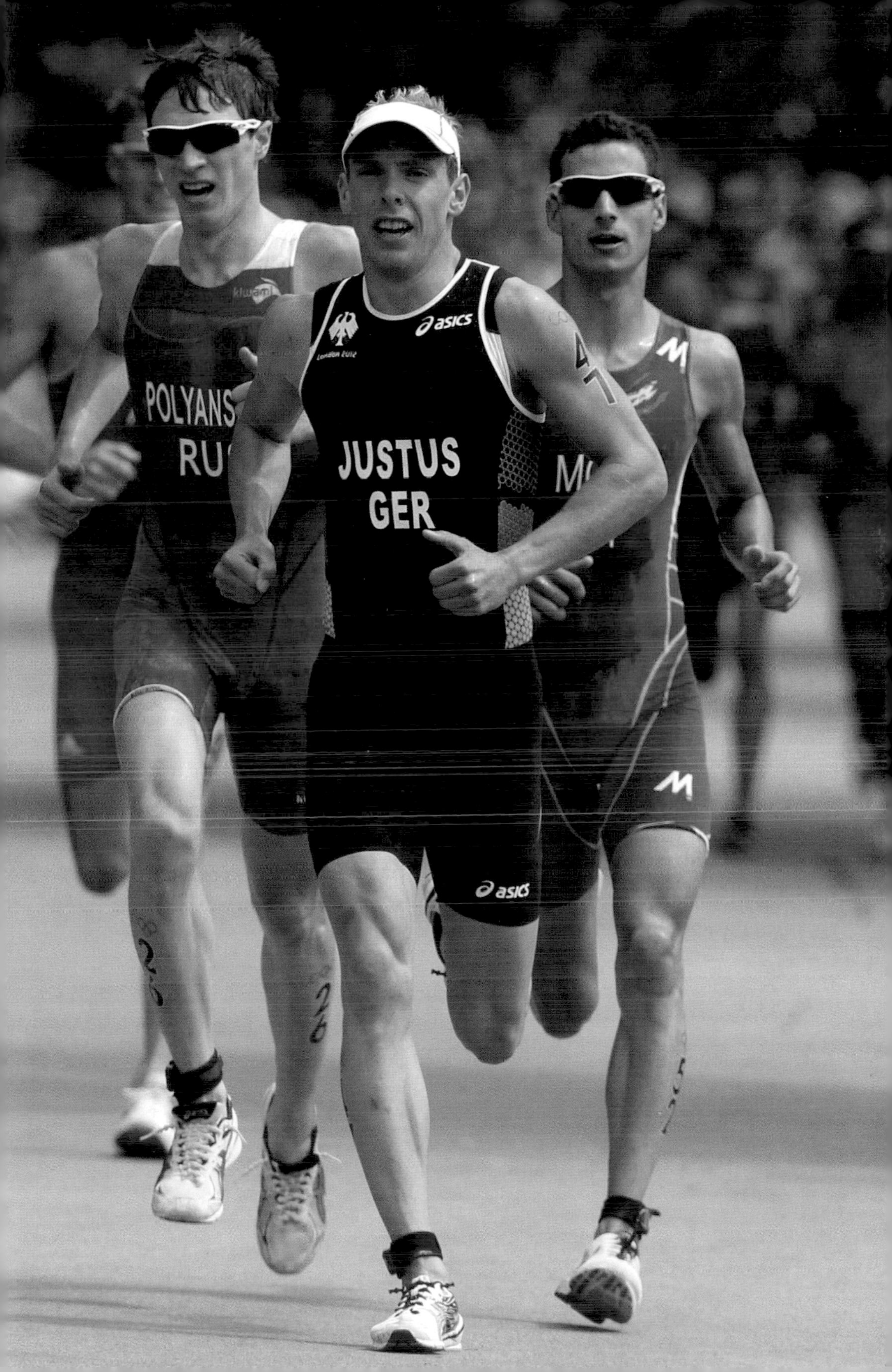
POLYANS
RUS
JUSTUS
GER
asics
London 2012
kiwami
asics

Next is your 'week at a glance' form. It enables you to plan a week's training in advance built around what the detailed availability planner above tells you.

This example shows the outline of your week with rough outlines of where the sessions will be. It includes a massage session, but this could be replaced by a pilates class, aerobics or simply a stretching session at home.

PLANNING FORM EXAMPLE – YOUR WEEK AT A GLANCE

	Swim	Bike	Run	Transition	Other
Mon	a.m.		p.m.		p.m.
Tue		p.m.	lunch		
Wed	a.m.	p.m.			p.m.
Thu			p.m.		massage
Fri	a.m.	p.m.			a.m.
Sat			a.m.	p.m.	
Sun	p.m.	a.m.			

Finally comes the session planner, which will be needed for each session that you do. The more detail you record the more useful these forms will be.

Opposite is an example of a cycling sessions plan. It may seem a little bit excessive to draw a session plan up each time but it is important that each session has a structure and an objective. This is best achieved by having a session plan.

PLANNING FORM EXAMPLE – SESSION PLAN

Day	Saturday	**Discipline**	Cycling
Time	9.00 a.m.	**Location**	South of town

Warm-up	20 min progressive ride out
Main body	90 min Including 3 × 10 min max effort 15 min between each effort
Cool down	20 min ride home
Stretching	Full legs and back
Comment	

SWIMMING

GETTING HELP TO IMPROVE

More than any other discipline, swimming relies on good technique. This book can't turn you into a fantastically efficient swimmer, but it does suggest *drills* and exercises that will help you improve; these are covered in the 'Technique training' section of this chapter (see pp. 25–30). If technique is the factor most holding you back then it is probably advisable to seek out some help. This help can come in a number of forms.

Swimming/triathlon clubs

A good club will run sessions that are supervised by a qualified and experienced coach. The coach should have a very active role, and if you go along to watch a session you should see them offering feedback to the swimmers and sometimes offering individual drills to help them improve. If you do join one of these sessions make sure the coach is aware of your goals, especially if you go to a swimming club – rather than a club specifically for triathlons – so that they can offer the right kind of help.

Personal swimming/triathlon coach

A much more expensive option, but one that can deliver rapid results. The individual *national governing bodies* can help you find a coach. Again, it is important once you have found a coach that you are clear about your goals.

Friend with video

This option will allow you to see how you swim. This can be fascinating and informative in equal measure. Get your friend or helper to film you as you swim a warm-up and a variety of distances. This will expose flaws in your style (for example, if your stroke deteriorates when you get tired). Once you have the film you can watch your stroke and compare it to those of other swimmers. There are lots of examples on the internet of world-class swimmers and triathletes, and the way they move through the water will help form a template for you to improve.

PERFORMANCE ASSESSMENT

Assessing where you currently are in your development is one of the key principles of this book. On the face of it this may appear to be a simple task: you can simply get into a swimming pool, swim a set distance and check how

long it takes. However, there a few things that need to be considered as you do this, to ensure you get a good idea of the way in which you swim/race so you can work on your weaknesses while reinforcing your strengths – another key principle. The first thing to do is to accept that in order for performance assessment to be reliable and repeatable, you will need to assess yourself in a swimming pool. Open-water swimming is a key part of triathlon and one that attracts and discourages equal numbers of people. You can complete some testing in open water and must be competent at swimming in this environment in order to race in it, but for the purposes of testing your technique and basic speed, a swimming pool will be necessary. The pool will probably need to be laned and relatively quiet to enable you to complete set tasks without encountering too much traffic. You will also need somebody to take your times so you can focus on swimming, though if you haven't got anyone available a watch and a good memory will probably suffice. You can extend the protocol below to include as many interim distances as you want but the key ones for development are every 100 metres. The beauty of this system is that it also allows you to extend the total distance upwards as far as is required. So for a super-*sprint* triathlon it may be 400 metres in total, but for a longer distance you will need to spend a much greater length of time in the water. This method uses what is known as *best pace*.

At the start of the test you will establish the distance you are going to cover and the intervals at which you will record times. For example:

750 metres in total. Timings taken at:
- 100 metres
- 200 metres
- 300 metres
- 400 metres
- 500 metres
- 600 metres
- 700 metres
- 750 metres

If you are going to race over multiple distances or have multiple goals in this area then repeat this test on different days but always make sure you are well rested, ideally with a rest day in swimming the day before the test. Make sure you complete a set warm-up. This should be around 300–400 metres of steady swimming. Rest for a few minutes then start the test. Pacing yourself is a key part of the test and will probably require practice.

Once mastered this test will give you a really good indication of the profile of your swimming. Are you fast to start? Do you struggle with distance? Is pacing an issue? All of these things will influence the way you need to train.

Work through the following example:

Andy did a run yesterday and hasn't had a swim for two days. His test is early in the morning with the help of a fellow simmer who is going to record his times for him. Andy swims his 400-metre warm-up starting gently but increasing his pace as he goes through. He uses a couple of different strokes and has a bit of a stretch after 300 metres. He is targeting a local open-water *sprint distance* triathlon later in the year and is therefore going to swim 750 metres as quickly as he can. His results are:

Distance in metres	Time
100	1.40
200	3.14
300	4.51
400	6.20
500	8.00
600	9.51
700	11.45
750	13.30

What does this show us? Andy starts well and his times in the first 400 metres are fast. After this he starts to slow a little. This could indicate several issues:

- Pacing could be a problem;
- Andy may not have experience with swimming at speed over these distances;
- Andy's technique may deteriorate as he gets tired;
- Andy may just be running low on energy at the later stages.

All of these issues can be resolved once identified and as you read this chapter you will see how to identify and work on the weaknesses you find. Below are some potential fixes for these and other issues you may find as you do your test:

- **Pacing could be an issue:** this will be ironed out by doing the test more often. Experience is the key to getting this right. It may also indicate that a swimmer goes too hard at the start of an event either through nerves or excitement.
- **Andy may not have experience with swimming at speed over these distances:** experience will come with time. Often a confidence issue, so more time in the pool training at or over race and target distance will help here.
- **Andy's technique may deteriorate as he gets tired:** this is a more difficult one to spot and to tackle. If the person you used to time you feels confident enough to do so they may be able to make a suggestion as to how you can improve. Sometimes video can be used to look at your own technique or you may need the help of a local coach or club to help you identify where you can improve your technique.
- **Andy may just be getting tired and running low on energy:** again, this an experience issue, as well as one of basic fitness that will be improved by the conditioning of the other disciplines as well as swim-specific training.
- **Swimmers may find that they go faster towards the end of a swim or test:** this can be a result of an insufficient warm-up, especially if the swimmer actually feels better as the swim goes on (this is more common in longer swims). It may also be the case that the swimmer was a little too conservative in the initial part of the swim and a better pacing strategy is required.
- **Swimmers may produce erratic times:** this can be caused by lack of concentration and therefore a greater focus on the task will help.
- **The time isn't as quick as you had hoped for:** improving your time is the very purpose of training!

You now have an idea of your current position and a method that can be repeated in a controlled environment to enable you to assess your progress on a regular basis. The circumstances around any test must be noted to ensure they are replicated, as a hard week at work, underlying illness or injury or poor nutrition may all impact upon testing, especially as you get fitter and the gains become smaller.

GOAL-SETTING

As this is the first discipline both in this book and in the event we will tackle the wider issues of goal-setting here. The principles of goal-setting can be applied to the event in its entirety, and to each discipline and individual training sessions. Well-constructed goals can motivate and inspire, poorly constructed goals can prove depressing and sometimes lead to abandonment of the event. A good goal must be:

- Specific
- Measureable
- Achievable
- Realistic
- Timed

Specific

'I will complete a triathlon'. As a goal this may seem acceptable but it hasn't stipulated what kind of event, distance or terrain you will attempt. It also doesn't stipulate if completion is the only goal or if there is a speed element to the goal. It doesn't matter if there is but, as this is the *Go Faster Guide*, we will assume that there is a target time. A better example of a goal would be, 'I will complete the Windsor *Standard Distance Triathlon* in less than three hours'.

A short-term set of targets may be, 'I will swim 750 metres in under 15 minutes by the end of May and in under 12 minutes by the end of July'.

Measureable

There must be no ambiguity about your goals. It is important to be able to tell whether or not you are improving: this is why a target time is useful, because you can see how you are progressing, rather than merely knowing that you have or haven't achieved your goal.

Achievable/Realistic

This is one for your own conscience though you do need to be sensible. Your goals must be well constructed so as to be achievable given the kind of training you can commit to and the type of event you are targeting. You may need some help on this one and it will very much depend on your level of previous activity and experience and your ability to commit to training. Getting quicker is often a case of quality rather than quantity so if you have targeted a faster race this may not be as difficult as you imagine, though again it depends on the time you want to achieve and how quickly you want to improve.

Timed

In our examples above you will see that there are clear timeframes to the reworded goals. The initial goal of completing a triathlon didn't specify when this would be done and as such it can remain on your 'to-do' list forever. Writing down what you want to achieve and when is very important.

Having established that you need goals, and what the structure of these goals will be, you now need to be bold enough to develop them. I would suggest that overall you have a goal such as:

- Complete my club's sprint distance race in July this year in under 1 hour 5 minutes.

In order to break this goal down for the swimming component we need to complete the test above (750-metre swim test), then set some goals for the swim-specific component of the triathlon. In the example of Andy, above, the overall time was 13.30. A reasonable set of target times may be:

Date	Target time
1 May	12.55
1 June	12.30
1 July	11.50

These may not seem like huge gains but remember that your goals must be realistic and achievable and should remain motivating throughout, with testing done monthly.

TECHNIQUE TRAINING

As I mentioned at the start of this section, swimming is highly technical. There are many books on the market that have high levels of illustration and include technical diagrams. This can be helpful but often doesn't add a great deal to the understanding of the individual. We have already discussed the use of video, which will be helpful in letting you see where you are and what your swimming should look like. The drills below will help you refine your swimming and any session should include a section where you apply one or two of the drills below. Pick the drills that best help tackle any issues that have been identified or that you feel you may have. If you are just looking to polish your technique, mix these drills through to keep some variety in your swim sessions.

Pool-swimming drills

Distance per stroke (DPS)

Getting maximum distance per stroke is helpful because using fewer strokes gives a more powerful and efficient style. In freestyle emphasise a long body-line, rotating both hip and shoulder, minimising resistance. Steady the rhythm, and always leave your front arm outstretched in the glide position until the trailing arm arrives, in what is called swimming in the front quadrant of the stroke. Use a set distance, preferably one length or more, and count the strokes you do. Try to use fewer strokes each time.

Fist swimming

Swim with your hands in fists. No 'karate-chop' hands allowed! Concentrate on body position, using your forearm in the *catch point* and optimum elbow bend through the stroke. When you return to swimming with an open palm, your hands will feel as large as kickboards! Have fun and keep thinking about your distance per stroke.

Sculling

Sculling is performed by sweeping your hands through the water, holding your elbows still. Your hands act like propeller blades, and subtle changes in hand angle and speed will change your body position and speed. There is no recovery motion. When you are treading water, you are sculling your hands through the water to hold yourself up and counteract gravity. To propel yourself down the pool, simply change your hand and forearm angle to be perpendicular to the pool bottom and parallel with the pool walls. Keep your elbows high at the surface of the water, and sweep your hands underneath (this is known as the 'windshield wiper' drill). Note that your swimming strokes are a combination of sculling motions that allow you to hold the water as your large body-core muscles act as the engine. This will help you best utilise your hands and lower arms and give you really strong feel for the water.

Kicking

Kicking without a kickboard will allow you to perform your kick in the same body position as the stroke. Kick on your side with your bottom arm (i.e. the one closer to the bottom of the pool) extended straight out of your shoulder-line in front of your head. Keep your palm facing down and your extended hand about 20 cm under water. Your top arm (the one on the surface of the water) should be relaxed at your side with your hand on your hip and out of the water. Maintain a head position as though you were swimming freestyle, with your head in line with your spine. Press your armpit toward the pool bottom to get your hip at the surface of the water. Your extended arm should feel weightless.

4/6/8-count drill

Kick on your side for a count of 4, 6 or 8 kicks. Take one full arm-stroke to rotate to your other side for another 4, 6 or 8 kicks, and continue through the swim. While on your side, focus on correct body position. When executing the switch, begin by lifting the elbow of the arm on the water surface (top arm) and recovering it over the line of your body. The extended arm (bottom arm) stays extended to maintain a streamlined body position, until the elbow of the top arm has passed over your head. Then execute a quick switch to your opposite side. Use core body muscles to rotate, while maintaining a hold on the water with your bottom arm.

Catch-up drill

When swimming full catch-up freestyle, pull with one arm at a time and touch your hands in a streamlined position out front between each alternating arm-stroke. Keep your extended hands about 20 cm under the surface of the water for improved body position. Concentrate on swimming in the front quadrant and keep a long, streamlined body-line.

You can progress to simply exchanging hands in the 'passing zone' extended in front. This is called the 'ear catch-up' drill, because you begin your pull as your opposite arm passes by your ear near the completion of the recovery. These drills will help you develop a more efficient, powerful stroke.

Fingertip-drag drill

This drill is swimming normal freestyle while dragging your fingertips along the surface of the water on the recovery phase of the stroke (i.e. when you move your arm out of the water to return it into the water in front of you). Focus on a high-elbow recovery, which ensures proper hand and elbow position at your hand entry. You should also check your body position during this drill, focusing on good side-to-side rotation. An alternate version of this drill involves dragging the entire hand, wrist-deep, through the water. This helps build the strength and speed of the arm recovery motion.

Gallop drill

This is the same as the 6-count drill above, but you take three strokes as you switch from side to side. Focus on long strokes and quick hips in these three strokes, completely rotating from one side to the other. Maintain perfect body position while kicking on your side.

Single-arm (R, L) drill

Single-arm freestyle swimming can be done in one of two ways.

- **Preferred:** with the opposite (non-working) arm at your side, breathe to the side of the non-working arm by turning your head away from the wave you have created. The secret to success with this drill is to complete your breath before stroking. Concentrate on the catch, initiating body rotation with the core body muscles. Take this drill slowly: technique is more important than speed.

- **Old-school:** with the opposite (non-working arm) extended in front, breathe to the side of the working arm. Focus on high-elbow recovery, hand entry and hand acceleration.

Rhythm drill

Single-arm freestyle with the opposite arm at your side (see description above), executing two right arms then two left arms. This takes some practice, but may very well become your favourite freestyle drill once you master it. Focus on rhythm and timing from the hips. Remember to take your breath with an arm extended out front (on the opposite side of the extended arm). If you can swim this drill easily and well, your technique is close to perfect.

Open-water swimming drills

Sighting drill

Swim normal freestyle. On every fifth stroke, raise your head straight forward and 'sight' on an object off in the distance. You can position your own target object or sight something already in place, for example a tree. After sighting the object, lower your head back into normal position. Practise maintaining a balanced stroke rhythm and rotation while keeping the target object in view.

Blind swimming

Swim normal freestyle with your eyes completely closed. On every fifth stroke, raise your head straight forward and 'sight' on an object in the distance (see above). Make sure you are maintaining a straight path down the pool. You can do this drill swimming side-by-side with your lane-mates to reinforce swimming in a straight path.

Deep-water start

This involves treading water while holding a position and then moving to a forward motion. Many mass-start races begin like this and as such it is a skill that needs to be practised and perfected so you get the best possible start to the race. The most effective way of doing this is to duck under the water quickly and allow your natural buoyancy to propel you upwards, kick hard and then start the arm stroke; this will pull you forward quickly.

SESSION PLANNING

Structuring your sessions will help you to build the programme that will make you a faster triathlete. The scheduling of these sessions will build into a programme that gives a sufficient load of training to stimulate improvement in condition and fitness balanced with the rest and recuperation that facilitates the improvement. The basic principle of training is called the overcompensation model (see the 'General workout/recovery cycle' diagram).

The theory behind this is that you apply overload by training. You recover by resting and the body's response to this is to supercompensate as it works harder than usual in order to anticipate the stress of training, so your fitness and condition are improved.

The key to this is recognising that in order to overcompensate it is necessary to rest. Therefore, it is essential that there is sufficient rest within a programme to facilitate the recovery process. This varies from individual to individual and generally as we age recovery takes longer. Other factors affecting the recovery process are: nutrition, *hydration*, overall fitness, overall health and pressures from everyday life. For example if you have trained hard in a session before

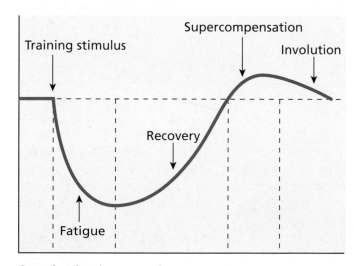

General workout/recovery cycle.

work, then perform a demanding or physical job, then try to train in the evening you will probably feel a little jaded and won't perform at your best. You may not have sufficiently recovered and doing this continuously won't progress your fitness and can often lead to illness or injury. I will look at nutrition and hydration more closely in Chapter 6.

So what do you need to consider as you structure your swimming session? Take a look at the session planning form overleaf; this will guide you through the process.

PLANNING FORM EXAMPLE – SESSION PLAN			
Day	Saturday	**Discipline**	Swimming
Time	9.00 a.m.	**Location**	Moana Pool
Warm-up	10 min progressive swim using mixed stroke and building *intensity* until breathing rate is elevated		
Main body	25 m catch up 25 min recovery × 400 m 2 × 50m as hard as possible 1 min rest – repeat building distance by 25 m each time until you are doing 200 m flat out. 1 min rest.		
Cool down	10 min easy swimming		
Stretching	Full legs and back		
Comment			

You may not think it is important to record the time and location but this information will be helpful to reflect back on when you review these sessions.

Warm-up

This part of the session is vital, do not skip it. A warm-up is important to prepare the mind and body for the activity ahead. The length of the warm-up can vary depending on:

- **environment and water temperature:** a cooler environment requires a longer warm-up;
- **intensity of the session planned:** a harder session needs a longer warm-up;
- **experience of athlete:** inexperienced athletes should warm up for longer;
- **age of athlete:** older athletes should warm up for longer.

The structure of the warm-up should involve a progressive set of activities to prepare you for the session ahead. In the case of swimming, this will involve gradually increasing the intensity of the swim as you progress. The shortest warm-up would be just under 10 minutes progressing from a very gentle stroke to a fuller stroke with greater physical and technical intensity. If the session is to include hard intervals, increase this time and take the intensity up to just under that which you anticipate doing in the main body of the sessions.

Main body

This is where you achieve the objective you have set yourself. Every session must have a session objective. Many triathletes don't set objectives and when questioned about why they do a specific session are unable to answer. You need to be able to explain, even if only to yourself, why you are working this hard and doing these specific exercises. For example, if you have recognised a weakness in your stroke you will have identified a matching drill to address the weakness. If you are working on increasing speed or stamina you will be addressing this through interval work or *endurance* and steady-state sessions. Potential fitness building sessions include:

Steady-state distance swimming
Important for building confidence and ingraining good habits. Swims of distances up to and beyond race distance are an important part of your programme.

Speed sessions
Building speed is best done using *interval training* (see below).

Cool-down

A simple reverse of the warm-up process that can encompass stretching in the pool if required. Using a gentle but stretching stroke to start with and gradually reducing the length and intensity of the stroke over a period of 5–10 minutes followed immediately by some static stretching of the arms, upper back and shoulders will be sufficient to ensure that you give the body the best possible chance of recovering from the sessions as quickly as possible.

DESIGNING TRAINING SETS

When constructing swimming training sets, the following 'DIRT' variables should be used and controlled.

- **D:** Distance (e.g. 100 metres, 200 metres, 400 metres);
- **I:** Interval of rest: always use a turnaround time (i.e. the time spent waiting to start the next length) in preference to rest interval, this way you control the speed of the swim and the amount of rest;
- **R:** Repetitions (number of times you repeat the exercise, e.g. 20, 30, 40);
- **T:** Time: a target for how quickly to achieve each repetition. This is obviously related to intensity and swim speed and should be based on the personal best time of the swimmer for a given distance. The closer the swimmer swims to their personal best times, the more demanding the level of intensity. The further away from the best time, the lower the level of intensity. The important thing to remember is that by asking yourself to achieve your best time you are controlling the effort of your swim.

By controlling the above variables, training sessions can be produced which give you control of volume, duration, intensity, rest and speed. The sets are measurable and can be logged and evaluated by both the swimmer and the coach (if you have one). The above set construction lends itself to the application of training overload and progression. The table below gives an example.

DIRT TRAINING SETS		
January	**March**	**May**
D = 100 m	100 m	100 m
I = @ 90 sec	@ 85 sec	@ 85 sec
R = 20×	20×	30×
T = hold 69 sec	hold 67 sec	hold 65 sec

Once you are familiar with the DIRT principles of training, it is relatively simple to alter each component to achieve a desired physiological training effect. Most physiologists agree that the main training areas suitable for manipulation are:

Endurance maintenance
This involves a long steady swim.

Endurance overload
This involves swimming more than the distance you will be racing but at a slower pace. This type of training is not essential, and can be undertaken infrequently (say every four to six weeks) or, if necessary, dispensed with altogether.

Lactate threshold
Your body produces *lactic acid* when you are working so hard that you can no longer supply sufficient oxygen to the muscles to meet the demands you are placing on it. *Lactate threshold* is the point at which your body is not able to recycle lactic acid sufficiently fast, and you start to accumulate it in the muscles. This will eventually hinder performance and cause a burning sensation in the muscles. The aim is to work so hard that you are generating lactic acid but not so hard that your body is not able to recycle it fast enough to prevent accumulation, and this is where lactic threshold training comes in. You can use a waterproof heart-rate monitor to establish your lactate threshold when swimming, but you will need to take measurements for all three disciplines, as your threshold may vary for different activities. You can then construct training

sessions to target improvements. Lactate threshold training is, simply put in the context of an endurance event like triathlon, exercising at the hardest intensity you can maintain. If you train around this intensity, you will make both the cardiovascular system and the muscles involved in the exercise you are doing more efficient. Training to increase your lactate threshold can make you a very effective athlete.

The principles of interval training discussed on p. 41 can be applied when targeting training for lactate threshold. First you need to try to establish what kind of level and intensity will be required to achieve this so we can build intervals based upon this intensity. To measure the intensity of this many people use heart-rate monitors and, increasingly for running and cycling, power meters. Using this equipment will help you train more accurately but it is not essential.

Using heart-rate monitors

Training to develop lactate threshold is determined by your lactate threshold heart rate, or number of heartbeats per minute to reach that level. The aerobic base (i.e. the point when lactic acid is not being produced) is usually around 65–75 per cent of that rate. Some use a formula, usually 220 minus their age, to figure out their lactate threshold, but really this is so vague and general as to be useless. To determine your own lactate threshold heart rate, purchase a heart-rate monitor and set aside 30 minutes for a field test. Set the monitor at the beginning of the trial and push yourself, but without training so hard that you slow down at the end. If you're not in the best of shape you might want to start the first 10 minutes easily and work your way up to your maximum heart rate. You can determine your own lactate threshold heart rate by figuring the average heart rate over the 30-minute time trial.

Of course this won't be 100 per cent scientifically accurate but it will be close enough to determine your own aerobic base. If your lactate threshold heart rate is 120, then you want to be working at 65–75 per cent of that, or 78–90 beats, for as long as possible. This develops your aerobic base and strengthens your heart and lungs. This test needs to be repeated for the running section as the heart rate will not necessarily be the same so you will need to revisit this in that chapter.

Sprint speed

If we define a sprint as a short (up to 60-second) burst of speed and intensity, then on first glance it may not seem important to develop this skill for triathlon. However, there are a number of situations in a race where sprint efforts will be tactically useful. Therefore you should aim to develop the ability to sprint when required by practising short intense bursts of effort (around 5–25 seconds should be enough).

Training targets

The training target is obviously related to the event. For example sprinters would do more *anaerobic* and speed work with less endurance-based training. Endurance-based athletes would do a higher percentage of aerobic endurance and lactate threshold work with less emphasis on speed and anaerobic work. Below are some criteria for constructing sets for each training area.

Criteria for endurance maintenance set construction

- Distance: 2000–8000 m or 20–90 min;
- Intervals: light; short rest intervals, i.e. 5–30 sec;
- Repetitions: any distance can be used;
- Timing: approximately 3–4 sec per 100 m slower than your threshold endurance.

Criteria for endurance overload set construction

- Distance: 1500–2000 m or 20–25 min;
- Intervals: rest intervals of 30–90 sec;
- Repetitions: repeat every 100–1500 m;
- Time: 2 sec per 100 m faster than endurance threshold; aim for the fastest possible average throughout the set.

Criteria for lactate threshold set construction

- Distance: 2000–3000 m or 25–40 min;
- Intervals: rest intervals of 10–30 sec;
- Repetitions distance: repeat every 2500–3000 m;
- Time: at individual 'anaerobic threshold'; maintain maximum even pace for the duration of the set (25–40 min).

Criteria for lactate production set construction

- Distance: 200–500 m per set, with 1–3 sets per training session;
- Intervals: rest intervals of 1–4 min;
- Repetition: repeat every 25–75 m;
- Speed: as fast as possible (approximately 98 per cent of your season's

best time), with maximum intensity and a suggested mileage per week of 1000–3000 m.

Criteria for sprint speed set construction
- Distance: 200–300 m, with 1–2 sets per session;
- Intervals: rest intervals of 30 sec–5 min;
- Repetitions: repeat every 10–50 m (including starts and turns);
- Time: maximum and faster than race pace.

ENERGY SYSTEMS

When an individual starts to exercise, the anaerobic energy system is accessed first. The main source of energy for this system is phosphocreatine. This system is immediate and short-lived, lasting for 10 seconds or so. During this period of time, the body does not actually require any oxygen, and neither lactic acid nor carbon dioxide are produced as a waste product. The glycolytic system is the second system that will be used. This is not as short-lived as the anaerobic system, and can last for up to 60–70 seconds. This is similar to the anaerobic system, in that it works without oxygen. However, unlike the anaerobic system, lactic acid is produced as a waste byproduct.

A 400-metre runner, for example, would be using the anaerobic and much of the glycolytic system during a race. When he crosses the finishing line, the levels of lactic acid in the muscles will be very high and will be burning.

If we pass the 60–90 second mark, the next system that will be used will be the aerobic system. This is when your body can produce vast amounts of adenosine triphosphate (ATP) to deliver sufficient oxygen to sustain your level of work, so the build-up of lactic acid is minimal. Fat and carbohydrate are

used as fuel, with fat used in greater amounts than carbohydrates. This system is very slow in comparison to the other two systems, and has a slow turnover of energy production allowing an athlete to work for a prolonged period of time using this system.

As intensity increases the body will move through the aerobic system to the anaerobic systems. It is worth remembering this and being aware that increases in intensity will rely on different methods of producing energy and propelling the body. A term that is frequently used is 'threshold'. This refers to the limit of aerobic capacity or the highest intensity you can sustain before your body needs to use the anaerobic energy system. This is important as the higher the intensity you can sustain without relying on the anaerobic systems the more efficient you will be and you can go faster for longer.

INTERVAL TRAINING

Interval training is used in all the disciplines and the principle remains the same across all three. You need to swim faster for a short period to get used to swimming faster and get the body conditioned to do it more often. By extending the period, but having sufficient rest you will get faster overall. You can increase the amount of time you spend doing the activity and balance this out with rest periods to help you progress. For example:

- Week 1: Swim 100 m as hard as possible, 1 length easy 30-sec rest.
- Week 2: Swim 150 m as hard as possible, 1 length easy 30-sec rest.
- Week 3: Swim 200 m as hard as possible, 1 length easy 30-sec rest.
- Week 4: Swim 200 m as hard as possible, 1 length easy.
- Week 5: Swim 250 m as hard as possible, 1 length easy.
- Week 6: Swim 300 m as hard as possible, 1 length easy.

All of these intervals should be repeated at least twice with the maximum number being set by your desired race distance. If you find the times of the intervals don't match the targets you set for yourself based on your objective, reduce the distance or number of intervals until it does and then structure your sessions from there. As you get stronger you will be able to swim closer to your target time and will have the ability to do more repetitions until you find at your next test that you have got quicker overall. While all three disciplines are reliant on technique to some extent, in swimming it is so vital that it can have a major impact upon your ability to get faster. If you are struggling with your technique, you may need to seek expert swim coaching advice. Despite this you can still progress to a certain point using these principles.

Scheduling a balance of fitness work and technique work into any session in a creative way, so you keep mentally as well as physically stimulated, is the key to adhering and succeeding with training. It is generally accepted wisdom that you do some technique drills first, straight after warm-up, then you do fitness work before entering the final phase of the session. You can alter this if you choose to but be aware that trying to ingrain good technique on a stroke when you are fatigued is often more difficult.

SCHEDULING SESSIONS

Bear in mind that because triathlon offers the opportunity to train in three sports instead of one, it is not uncommon for athletes to try and train as if they were a 1500 m swimmer, 40 km time trialler and a 10 km runner and sustain volumes that one might find in single sports. The outcome, unsurprisingly, is overuse injury! You can't possibly train really hard and really long in all three disciplines every day. As I am focusing on one specific discipline here, I will look at the scheduling of just the swim sessions in a week and a month. I will build this into a bigger picture as the book progresses.

Firstly you need to consider how often you are training. See the table below for rough guidelines.

SWIM SESSION SCHEDULING	
Number of sessions per week	**Suggested session types in week**
2 (minimum)	1 speed session 1 endurance session
3	2 speed sessions 1 endurance session
4	2 speed sessions 2 endurance sessions
5	3 speed sessions 2 endurance sessions
6	3 speed sessions 2 endurance sessions 1 recovery swim

The sessions should be spread out throughout the week and consideration should be given to the time of day at which you are training (based on your personal preferences; everyone's energy levels are different throughout the day). If you have an open week your sessions could look like this:

THREE SESSIONS					
	Swim	**Bike**	**Run**	**Transition**	**Other**
Mon	speed				
Tue					
Wed	endurance				
Thu					
Fri	speed				
Sat					
Sun					

FOUR SESSIONS

	Swim	Bike	Run	Transition	Other
Mon	speed				
Tue	endurance				
Wed					
Thu	speed				
Fri	endurance				
Sat					
Sun					

FIVE SESSIONS

	Swim	Bike	Run	Transition	Other
Mon	speed				
Tue	endurance				
Wed	speed				
Thu					
Fri	endurance				
Sat	speed				
Sun					

The time of the sessions should be looked at carefully so you are not forcing your body to swim late at night and then again early the next morning. This would probably be asking a little too much of yourself.

Recording your session

The comment section of the session plan is useful to allow you to make some observations about yourself and the session you have done. This will help when you look back on the sessions as a log of your activity either shortly after or more often many months after to review how you succeeded against your goals, or how you didn't.

EQUIPMENT

The equipment requirements for swimming may appear to be simple. However, proper care taken when selecting the right kit for training and racing will enhance the experience in both.

Swimming costume

The vast majority, if not all, of the training will be done in a swimming pool, so obviously you'll need a swimming costume! For men the choice will be between a close-fitting pair of swim trunks and looser-fitting swim shorts. The closer-fitting garment is the best option as it will provide less resistance and will allow the development of a good quality stroke without the hindrance of baggy materials. The choice for women is generally between a one- or a two-piece costume. A single-piece outfit is good, although there are two-piece outfits (some of which are triathlon-specific) that will be very comfortable and entirely suitable. Most swimmers will choose to wear swimming goggles. There is a huge array of

different goggle designs and colours and it may take a bit of experimenting to establish the best design for you. Goggles should be comfortable when snugly fitted, and the care of goggles, and indeed all the other equipment you will use, will play a large part in determining their longevity. Rinsing all equipment with clean fresh water will enhance their performance and lifespan. Many people use some form of footwear when walking around the swimming pool area. Flipflops can make the experience much more pleasant and prevent infections being passed on. Swimming hats are mandatory in some pools but may also be advantageous both for protecting your hair and improving performance. If you have longer hair you will definitely benefit from using a swimming hat, as this will prevent the distraction caused by hair moving across your face and interruption your stroke as well as providing resistance in the water. Swimming hats are cheap items to acquire, but they will also benefit from the same level of care as your other gear.

Floats

We have discussed a number of drills and activities to help you improve your swimming technique and performance. To complete these drills effectively you may need to use some form of float. There are two basic types of float: the pull buoy and the hand float.

The pull buoy is used between the legs to enhance buoyancy and enable the swimmer to concentrate on the arm function within the stroke. The hand float can be used in a number of ways but is generally employed to support the upper body when concentrating on improving leg action.

Paddles, fins and flippers can be used in some drills and can enhance the power of a swimmer. They are useful tools but some swimmers can start to rely on the sensation that they provide which can have a negative effect on overall swimming performance. If you think, after reading the information in this chapter, that you will benefit from using these tools then do so sparingly and as part of a balanced programme.

Wetsuit

Many triathlon events take place in open water. If you are planning on tackling this kind of event you will almost certainly need a *wetsuit*. There are some rules relating to the wearing of wetsuits.

If the temperature is below a certain point then wetsuits are compulsory. The temperatures and associated distances are:

- 13°C = maximum swim distance of 2000 m;
- 12°C = maximum swim distance of 1000 m;
- 11°C = maximum swim distance of 500 m.

There are also rules governing the wearing of wetsuits at the other end of the temperature spectrum, and wetsuits cannot be worn in the following temperatures:

- above 22°C in a race of less than 2000 m;
- above 23°C in a race of between 2000 m and 2999 m;
- above 24°C in a race of above 3000 m.

Because of average sea temperatures in the UK you are unlikely to be allowed to start an open water race without a wetsuit, and it is very unlikely that the water temperature will be high enough to prevent you from wearing one. If you are fortunate enough to race abroad then you will need to check the local weather conditions and take advice regarding the use of wetsuits.

Which wetsuit to use is an important decision. Wetsuits can be hired from a number of big companies, allowing the novice athlete to take part in an open water event without having to commit to an expensive purchase, which a good-quality wetsuit can easily be. If you decide you do want to purchase a wetsuit, either because you intend to participate in a number of events or because you have the facility to practise in open water then you will need some guidance. Triathlon magazines such as *220 Triathlon* carry a wide variety of triathlon-specific wetsuit advertisements. These wetsuits have been designed specifically for the demands of the sport and are cut appropriately around the arms to allow *flexibility* in a way often not found in a diving, skiing or generic watersports wetsuits. This is not to say you can't use these suits but you may find them considerably less comfortable.

There are also open water training venues where you will be able to get used to swimming in this environment; many of these venues have hire facilities.

CYCLING

CYCLING DISCIPLINES

Most people can ride a bike, but doing so in a triathlon is very different to what you may have done on your commute to work, or in the park as a child. For example, not only do you need to be able to ride as quickly as possible, you also need to learn to get a good running start from the bike for the transition to the running stage of the event.

A cursory understanding of the skills involved in cycling will open up and add variety to training sessions. Below are some disciplines that will help get you used to competitive cycling, with a brief explanation of how they will improve your abilities as a triathlete. If you are training for a *draft-legal* triathlon then you will need further techniques and tactics. Draft-legal events for non-professionals, while they are on the increase, remain fairly rare.

Track cycling

Carried out on hard banked tracks either indoors or outdoors, sometimes on grass, this kind of cycling uses a bike with a fixed gear and no brakes. This kind of riding smooths a rider's pedalling style, and develops *cadence* and ability to achieve and sustain high speeds for a relatively short space of time. The fixed *gears* and the safety of the environment mean it is also good for threshold training (see below) and intense work. Many tracks run drop-in sessions where you can hire a bike. If you want to move onto track racing proper you will need a racing licence from British Cycling.

BMX/cycle speedway

Very short races on specific bikes. Not many triathletes use this method, but it can be excellent for developing bursts of power and bike-handling skills. There are a number of good-quality BMX facilities around the country, and they are generally very welcoming to novices. Triathletes will learn skills that can be transferable through there is an inherent risk of minor falls within BMX riding. Clubs will help guide you should you decide to compete in BMX races.

Off-road cycling

This can take the form of mountain biking or cyclo-cross (an off-road cycle sport using bikes that look like road-race bikes but have lower gears and coarsely treaded tyres). Both of these forms of riding will develop aerobic ability, lactate threshold (see p. 36) and most importantly bike-handling ability. Cyclo-cross has a growing number of local leagues that can provide good motivating competition through the winter as well as helping riders learn how to ride better and handle crashes in a safe environment. Cyclo-cross and mountain-bike cross-country riding offer a lot to the triathlete, and are designed to be undertaken in poor conditions, even snow, meaning you can train all year round. The development in bike-handling skills can be a real reward, especially for triathletes who come from a non-cycling background. A racing licence will be required for most mountain-bike events though there will be a novice category in most larger races. Cyclo-cross is very easy to enter and the British Cycling website keeps details of these races, which typically take place between September and February. You can normally just turn up, enter and ride.

Road racing

Group riding on a standard road bike, with distances for novices from 25 to 100 km. The constantly changing pace will develop a rider's aerobic ability, lactate threshold and short-term power. Bike-handling will also improve. Entering this kind of event can be a bit daunting at first and many riders find their first experience of this kind of riding both terrifying and exhilarating in equal measure. Races are listed by British Cycling and often you can turn up and ride, though it does make sense to contact the organiser beforehand. Road racing is broken down into categories from fourth through to first. A fourth-category race is the most appropriate for novices. A racing licence is a good idea but you can get one to cover the race itself from the organiser if required.

Time trialling

Solo (though sometimes in small groups) riding on a standard road bike or specific time-trial or triathlon machine. Completing the course in the shortest possible time. Distances vary from 10 to 100 miles. Excellent training for non-*drafting* triathletes, this very accessible form of cycle sport best matches the demands of most triathlons and as such is excellent training for triathletes. To take part you need to be a member of a cycling or triathlon club that is affiliated to Cycling Time Trials (www.cyclingtimetrials.org.uk). The closest form of cycle sport to the demands of most triathlon and by far the cheapest.

PERFORMANCE ASSESSMENT

Firstly, you will need to look at your levels of fitness and performance, much as you did with swimming, though it is arguably more difficult as the environment in which cycling takes place is much less controlled than the swimming pool and as such meaningful testing can be difficult. Factor in the effects of the

weather, cold, wind, rain and traffic and safety considerations and this starts to look almost impossible. Even a *turbo trainer*, attached to a suitable device for measuring distance, still has a number of associated variables that you need to consider. For this reason we will look at two tests and some variables within them so you have something to track progress against.

Road-testing

It's difficult to be very prescriptive here as local conditions are key but you need to find a route, preferably a circuit, of a suitable distance. The distance will very much depend on the event you are targeting. If you are targeting a sprint event a route of around 45–60 minutes will be sufficient. Standard-distance athletes should target 75–90 minutes and long-distance athletes should target 2 hours or more, though you may need to do multiple repetitions as your planning progresses. Your route should be as quiet as possible, have no traffic lights on it and be as safe and technically unchallenging as possible so that you can concentrate solely on performance. After a warm-up (see p. 58 below) approach the start of your route from a rolling start and hold the best pace that you can. Once at best pace, hold it for the duration of your route. It is worth adding a couple of stopping points on the route at approximately 15-minute intervals so you can record your progress. You can use these points to assess your abilities over the relevant distance. For example, you can identify and address problems such as starting too quickly or tailing off towards the end. You may find it difficult to analyse your cycling as closely as you did your swimming as there may be external factors, such as hills and wind direction, which affect your time. When road-testing you may find it helpful to use a *power meter* as a measure of your ability (see p. 68 for more on using power meters).

Once you have completed the test, write the results down. If you are using a heart-rate monitor (see p. 72) record your average and maximum heart rate. If you are using a power meter you can download the information from your handlebar-mounted screen and save it as your power profile for the ride.

If you are targeting long-distance events you may find that a circuit of around 2 hours is useful. As you get closer to your event you can increase this and conduct longer tests by completing the route twice. It shouldn't be necessary to go much further than this in testing as there is no evidence that longer tests are useful other than to give confidence in covering the distance required. The protocols for a longer test remain the same and while the environmental factors will have a greater impact, simply because you are outside for longer, the information gathered will still be relevant and will give you a benchmark of your performance that can be used to compare subsequent rides on the same course.

Testing using a turbo trainer

Testing using a static turbo trainer can be easier than training on the road, because of the lack of traffic. However, there are still elements that need to be considered. The turbo trainer places a great deal of emphasis on physical conditioning, at the expense of handling skills, and the fact that there is no traffic is a double-edged sword as you will not improve your road awareness.

The resistance between the tyre and the turbo trainer via the roller must be consistent. Many turbo trainers have resistance controls and you can fine-tune the resistance using this. To get a basic useable calibration set the bike up and use the same tyre pressure as you do for normal road riding. Use a low to medium resistance that best seems to replicate riding on a fairly flat road. Once set up ride in any gear (though you must make a note of which you use) for 10 minutes at a cadence of around 80–100 rpm. Then increase cadence to 100 rpm, make a note of your speed and stop pedalling. Take a note of exactly how long it takes for the rear wheel to stop spinning as this will form part of how you repeat this test by creating similar conditions each time. This is a basic method but should give you the basis for a repeatable test, though it is important that the parameters remain the same in each test. When using a turbo it is essential that you use a fan to help cool the body, as you will not have the benefit of outside air temperature regulating your body heat. This can have an effect on the heart rate, making the test feel much harder than it would be outside., and you may notice higher average heart rates than for similar efforts outside.

Once you have set up your turbo and have recorded all the elements to ensure your test is repeatable you can set up for your test. Firstly your bike will need a wireless rear-wheel-mounted speed sensor. Some expensive turbo trainers have these fitted already. The following distances will be appropriate for different events:

- Sprint event 10 miles;
- Standard event 20 miles;
- Long distance 30 miles.

Longer tests on the turbo may be difficult to stay motivated for. You should warm up and then roll into the test by pedalling from a gentle speed and increasing steadily to the desired speed just before you start the test. Record the time taken to complete each mile and if possible record heart rate at each mile; this will enable you to calculate your average heart rate for the ride. If you are using a power meter, record average power and power at each mile. You can record your results in the following table.

TURBO TRAINER RECORD						
Mile	Time	Overall Time	Heart Rate	Average Heart Rate	Power Output	Average Power Output
1						
2						
3						
4						
5						
6						
7						
8						
9						
10						
11						
12						
13						
14						
15						
16						
17						
18						
19						
20						

This will give you a comprehensive set of data that is extremely useful. It will show you where you get tired, how well you pace yourself and what your average heart rate and power (if available) are.

Closed-road circuit testing

There are a number of closed-road cycle circuits across the UK, details of which can be found on the British Cycling website (www.britishcycling.org.uk). You can use one of these to compete your outside testing. The principles of testing in these environments are similar to on the open road, but with a degree of enhanced safety as there is no traffic. The wind is likely to have less overall effect because as you go around the circuit you alternate between riding into the wind (having to increase your efforts accordingly) and benefiting from having the wind behind you, pushing you along. You will also have to corner both into it and with it behind you, which is also a good skill to develop as it represents real-life road and racing conditions. If you live close to one of these circuits do consider using it.

TECHNIQUE TRAINING

You can apply the principles of developing fitness discussed in Chapter 2 to the discipline of cycling. Athletes who have experience of cycling clubs will no doubt have been made aware of the types of training available to them. The mainstay of most cycling clubs is the traditional morning club run. This type of training is predominantly long and steady, and will develop *aerobic fitness* (see p. 40). While training in a group is not the only way of developing this kind of fitness, group training will make it more tolerable as the duration involved (1.5–2 hours or more for medium-distance and 3.5 hours or more for long-distance racing) can be tedious for all but the most self-disciplined individuals. Group riding can be daunting and care should be taken when beginning to develop this unique aspect of cycling skill, but it is the best way of getting experience relevant to riding in a triathlon. You can get a list of clubs from your national governing body.

More intense training will be needed to develop the other areas of fitness that impact on cycling performance. Interval training should play an important part in the development of cycling performance, and by using the principles detailed in Chapter 2 you can develop your own interval training sessions effectively.

Warm-up

The considerations for a cycle warm-up are broadly similar to those in the pool. As cycling uses a smooth circular motion, you are warming muscles and getting your heart ready for the effort. It is worth experimenting to get a warm-up that suits you but it will be between 15 and 30 minutes. The temperature of the air will also have a big impact, as your muscles will be closer to operating temperatures on a warm day, but will need longer to warm up when the ambient temperature is low. An example of a 25-minute warm-up is given below:

- 4 minutes spinning gently increasing cadence to around 90 rpm;
- 10 minutes progressively increasing intensity to almost race/time trial levels;
- 2 minutes easy riding;
- 4 sets of 20-second sprints with 30–45 seconds between them;
- 5 minutes steady cycling at an intermediate intensity.

The first and second activities can be extended to accommodate factors such as temperature.

Testing frequency
Testing on the bike is probably not useful if done more than once a month. Schedule it in the same way you would with swimming by making sure you are well rested and haven't undertaken any intense rides in the preceding few days.

DESIGNING TRAINING SETS
The volume of cycling that you will need to do will depend very much on your target event. If you are completing an *ironman* event you will need much more endurance-based training compared to an athlete preparing for a sprint or even a standard-distance event. You should now have already established some basic data for your cycling and know how long, far and fast you can cycle and how long it takes to cover the distances you are targeting.

Use the 10 per cent rule as the basis for increasing the volume of your riding, i.e. only increase the amount of time spent on the bike by 10 per cent per week. This will help to prevent overtraining and injury.

The main training areas are the same as for swimming (see Chapter 2).

Endurance maintenance
This will involve the long steady type of ride described at the beginning of the chapter. These can be done in a group or alone and will vary depending on the event you are targeting. For a sprint triathlon, rides of 2 hours maximum are probably all that is required. For standard-distance events, 3 hours and for middle- and long-distance events rides of between 75 and 100 per cent of the time taken will be required. These rides do not need to be weekly but you need to be confident that you can cycle the distances involved and therefore regularly riding distances will be helpful, and will ingrain good technique.

Endurance overload
This involves riding more than the distance you will be racing but at a slower pace. As I said in Chapter 2, this type of training is not necessarily essential, but if you do undertake it, increase the times and distances suggested for endurance maintenance training.

Lactate threshold
When cycling, your lactate threshold is closely related to your functional threshold power, or FTP (see p. 65 for more on FTP).

Sprint speed
Sprint speed will be especially important in cycling in the following circumstances.

Exiting T1
The first transition phase, from swimming to cycling, is known as T1. A burst of speed will be required to get the bike moving. This should be of moderate intensity but must be sufficient to get moving and allow time for you to get feet

into shoes and settle into the ride. Practice would involve efforts of around a minute, repeated 2–5 times.

Cornering

It is important that you consider the physiological, as well as the technical, elements of cornering. You will almost certainly need to reduce speed to get around a corner. This means you will need to accelerate once you have exited the corner. These sprints can be from a very low speed, almost a standing start, to medium speed back up to high speed. Either practise corners or focus on the physical aspect and complete some shorter sprint intervals of 10, 20 or 30 seconds, where you accelerate from a slow or medium speed up to a high speed. Repetitions can be fairly high (3–10) and you may find that you are forced to rest. Don't worry, this accurately reflects a racing scenario, where corners come one after another on technically demanding circuits.

Hills

Many people don't see these as sprints but with the exception of much longer climbs over substantial hills and mountains most of the climbs we come across last around the level of time that we would consider a sprint. This kind of training is best done on the climbs themselves as positioning and technique do play a part. Repetitions can be low (2–4).

Overtaking

While many people wouldn't see this as a sprint, you should consider it as such as it is an increase in effort over a short period of time. Riding from a quick pace you should accelerate and hold for about one minute then drop back down to the previous race pace. This is very structured training and the key is to be able to drop back down to your previous pace and effort but not substantially below it, or you risk being immediately overtaken by the cyclist you just passed, which can be a bit embarrassing! Get this kind of training right and you will become much more effective in *non-draft*-legal races.

Attacking

Most appropriate for draft-legal races, in a situation where you are attacking a group to get a breakaway gap with the aim of staying away from that group. This involves sprinting then holding a high pace. You can practise this by starting at a moderate speed, sprinting, then holding a pace which is lower that your sprinting pace but higher than your moderate pace. Your sprint (breakaway) effort should last 30–60 seconds with a sustained period of hard effort (5 minutes) immediately afterwards. Often you would then return your pace to that of the group to maintain rather than increase the gap. As this is quite a structured and sustained effort one or two repetitions will probably be sufficient.

Speed training

If you are targeting a specific time then speed will be a major factor for you. You will need to know what average speed is necessary to achieve the time you want. Your initial testing (see above) will show you where you are, and once you have your target average you need to work out how far you are away from being able to do this speed over the distance required. This of course involves a test over the distance you plan to cover, followed by a simple bit of maths to establish your average speed. For example:

Distance	Time taken	Average speed
20 km	55 min	$(20/55) \times 60 = 21.8$ kph
40 km	80 min	$(40/80) \times 60 = 30$ kph
180 km	330 min	$(180/330) \times 60 = 32.7$ kph

This calculation can also be applied to miles and mph simply by altering these units. Having done this you will need to look to increase your average speed. To do this target short periods of time to accelerate to just above your target speed and hold it. Start with 2 minutes and then increase by 1 minute until you can hold 10 minutes at your desired pace. You need to have between 1 and 3 minutes easy riding between intervals to recover. So for example:

Set 1:
- 15 min warm-up (steadily increase the intensity over 15 min until you feel warm and ready to start);
- 2 min at 22 kph;
- 3 min very easy;
- complete the 2 min on 3 min off routine five times;
- 15-min cool-down (steadily decrease the effort with some light yet brisk pedalling).

Set 2:
- 15 min warm-up;
- 4 min at 22 kph;
- 2 min very easy;
- complete the 4 min on 2 min off routine seven times;
- 15 min cool-down.

Set 3:
- 15-min warm-up;
- 6 min at 22 kph;
- 1 minute very easy;
- complete the 6 min on 1 min off routine 10 times;
- 15-min cool-down.

If you have a large gap between your current speed ability and your target speed ability then you can repeat this process of overloading and developing speed in a number of stages. So, for example, you could complete the above which would take place over a number of weeks and build you up to being able to ride at 22 kph. Then start again with a target of 26 kph going back to Set 1 but using 26 kph not 22 kph. By going through this process with different speeds over a number of weeks and months you can build the ability to ride faster. You will also be developing your endurance by simply riding longer, which will contribute to your strength and speed as well. The terrain of your rides, both for training and competition needs to be carefully considered as this will have a major impact upon overall speed and race time. Most race organisers will give out information about the courses used, and training over similar terrain will be useful in terms of event specific preparation but training over varying distances and terrains is probably the most healthy way of developing your overall cycling skills and abilities.

Distance training

Distance training is essential for ability and confidence. For sprint- and standard-distance triathletes this could be the full distance raced, but it is not necessary for long-distance athletes to cover the full race distance in training; 75–100 per cent of the distance should suffice. You can then build the training of cycling around the principles of interval training, discussed in Chapter 2. Bear in mind that when cycling, rest intervals will be easy because the bike allows you to keep rolling with very little effort. The table below shows how DIRT principles can be applied to cycling.

DIRT TRAINING SETS			
	Jan	**Mar**	**May**
D	As far as you can in 2 min as hard as possible	4 min hard effort	5 min hard effort
I	30 sec	90 sec	90 sec
R	9	12	15
T	Hold 90 rpm pedalling speed	Hold 90 rpm	Hold 90 rpm

Skills training

Developing your skills work within cycling is often overlooked and as such it needs to be specifically scheduled in. It is a good idea to do some skills work as part of your warm-up then build another aspect of development into the main body of the session. This can be achieved by carefully planning your route and by ensuring that you are clear about what you are doing.

Interval training session examples

It is important to plan each individual session to get the most out of it. An example of a complete session involving skills work is given below.

SKILLS SESSION EXAMPLE			
Day	Monday	**Discipline**	Cycling
Time	6.00 p.m.	**Location**	Out of town 5 km circuit (repeat 4 times)
Warm-up	Ride out to circuit concentrating on achieving cadence of over 100 rpm after first 5 min.		
Main body	1 km as hard as possible, 2 km easy, repeat for duration of ride. Concentrate on gear selection by using at least 4 gears during the effort.		
Cool down	Repeat corners 3 and 4 on the circuit (turning back) 5 times each focus on body position and speed carried through the corner.		
Stretching	At home, stretch legs and back.		
Comment			

INTERVAL (SPEED) SESSION EXAMPLE			
Day	Wednesday	**Discipline**	Cycling
Time	6.00 a.m.	**Location**	Outer town 10-mile time trial course
Warm-up	Ride out picking up cadence in first 10 min until 100 rpm.		
Main body	10 miles as hard as can hold, 5 min easy × 3.		
Cool down	Ride back in very easy gear		
Stretching	At home, stretch legs and back.		
Comment			

INTERVAL (SPRINT) SESSION EXAMPLE

Day	Wednesday	Discipline	Cycling
Time	6.00 a.m.	Location	Hilly circuit

Warm-up	Ride out to circuit concentrating on cadence and building intensity
Main body	Use the short hill (20–30 seconds) and sprint out of the saddle in a gear that is hard but enables cadence of 80–95 rpm. Rest for 10 min (active) and repeat 4–8 times.
Cool down	
Stretching	At home, stretch legs, arms and back.
Comment	

Functional threshold power

Functional threshold power (FTP) is one of the key factors of training with power on the bike.

Functional threshold power is a much misunderstood phrase but if you apply it properly it will make you a fitter, faster, stronger cyclist.

It's generally agreed that your functional threshold power is the maximal power output you can sustain for the duration of 1 hour. This is not the same as your average power, which is calculated using all the fluctuations in your speed over the period of an hour. FTP is the power level you can maintain constantly for an hour.

Calculating your FTP is quite straightforward. If you've got power meter analysis software (generally supplied with your power meter) you can use your race and training data to accurately estimate your FTP through the normalised power function at the 60 minutes axis point. You could do a ramp test, a profile of which is seen here, and extrapolate the figures you need from its results. The final 60 seconds of sustained power are computed and your FTP will be approximately 75 per cent of this.

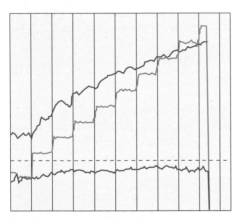

Graph of ramp test (blue = heart rate; green = power; red = pedal cadence).

A 20-minute test will give fairly accurate results, but the results of a 1-hour test (a 25-mile/40 km time trial) will be almost 100 per cent accurate.

To undertake a 20-minute test ride as hard as you can for 20 minutes (a 10-mile time trial), use the normalised power figure provided by your software, and you'll get 105 per cent of your functional threshold. It's not as accurate as a full hour test, but it's less stressful, easier to fit in to a busy schedule. Now that you have the figure for your functional threshold, you need to work on raising it.

As a triathlete, raising FTP should be your primary objective. You need to become more efficient at making use of your overall effectiveness. Here I'll explain why.

Two riders can have exactly the same relative VO_2max, but it will be the one with a higher FTP who prevails come race day.

Two club riders may turn out exactly the same power over the course of an hour, but their physical attributes, heart volume and lung capacity may differ so their heart rates could be miles apart. The power outputs and the lines on the wattage graph may be the same but their physiological response, sensations and emotions most definitely won't!

Power meter users often try to hit the big maximal power numbers to reflect the measure of their prowess on the bike. This won't necessarily be effective, as a cyclist who has a lower level of maximal power but sustains it for longer may prevail over a cyclist who can hit high levels of maximal power before dropping back down to a low power-level.

Functional threshold power gives you a baseline from which you can design your future training levels. Once you have enough power data to draw a conclusion, changing your FTP is pretty straightforward, and it is easy to track your progress.

Zones

If you are using a heart-rate monitor or power meter for cycling, you can use zones to schedule and target efforts during your training sessions. The following zones may prove useful.

POWER-BASED ZONES FOR CYCLING

Level	Name	Average Power	Average heart rate	Perceived Exertion	Description
1	Active recovery	<55%	<68%	<2	This is very low-level exercise: you are pedalling extremely lightly, and are able to have a conversation while doing so. You will not feel tired, and are unlikely to increase your fitness. Zone 1 is normally used for active recovery after strenuous training days, or in intervals between efforts.
2	Endurance	56–75%	69–83%	2–3	This is the pace for long, slow distance training. Effort and fatigue levels remain low, but may increase, for example when climbing a hill. You will only have to concentrate for the more strenuous parts of the ride, and should still be able to have a conversation. You can undertake Zone 2 training frequently, but a particularly long session may necessitate a day-long recovery.
3	Tempo	76–90%	84–94%	3–4	A brisk ride. More effort required than for Zone 2. You will have to concentrate to maintain continuous effort. Conversation will be somewhat halting, as you will have to breathe rhythmically and continuously. If your fitness level is right you may still be able to train consecutive days in Zone 3. This is the typical pace for *fartlek* workouts.

4	Lactate threshold	91–105%	95–105% (may not be achieved during initial phases of effort(s))	4–5	You. are constantly exerting moderate effort, and will feel accordingly fatigued The depth and frequency of breathing necessary will render conversation very difficult. A very high level of concentration is required, so training in 10–30-min blocks advisable. It is possible to train consecutive days in Zone 4, but only if you are very well rested.
5	VO$_2$max	106–120%	>106%	6–7	If you are training to increase your VO$_2$max, enter Zone 5 for 3–8-min intervals. Conversation will be impossible and you will feel extremely tired. You should only attempt Zone 5 training if you are well rested, and consecutive days of training are not advisable.
6	Anaerobic capacity	>121%	N/A	>7	Short (30-sec to 3-min), high intensity intervals designed to increase anaerobic capacity. You will feel extremely tired and will be unable to hold a conversation. Consecutive days of training not advisable.
7	Neuro-muscular power	N/A	N/A	* (Maximal)	Very short, very high intensity efforts (e.g. jumps, standing starts, short sprints), usually placing stress on musculoskeletal rather than metabolic systems.

HEART-RATE TRAINING ZONES FOR CYCLING

Heart rate zone 1	<65% maximum heart rate.	Recovery training
Heart rate zone 2	65–75%	Easy endurance training
Heart rate zone 3	75–85%	Moderate endurance training
Heart rate zone 4	85–90%	Solid endurance training
Heart rate zone 5	90–95%	Extensive interval training
Heart rate zone 6	>95 %	Intensive interval training

SCHEDULING SESSIONS

I have looked at the balance of training for swimming. The same considerations need to be taken when building the cycling programme. Top competitive cyclists can train for anything up to 30 hours per week. However, the triathlete must balance cycling training with other disciplines. Many factors will decide what emphasis you place on cycle training, chief among them how your cycling ability compares to your ability in the other two disciplines. Remember, the principles of training apply across the board. It would be unwise to perform a high-intensity workout in the pool followed by a similarly high-intensity workout running or cycling. With careful planning, sessions can be integrated.

Firstly you need to consider how often you are training. As a rough guideline:

Number of sessions per week	Suggested sessions types in week
2 (minimum)	1 speed/interval sessions
	1 endurance session combined with some skills
3	1 speed/interval session
	1 skills/interval session
	1 endurance session
4	2 speed/interval sessions
	1 skills/interval session
	1 endurance sessions
5	2 speed/interval sessions
	1 skills/interval session
	2 endurance sessions (one possibly recovery based)
6	3 speed/interval sessions
	1 skills/interval session
	2 endurance sessions (one possibly recovery based)

The sessions should be spread out throughout the week. If you have an open week your sessions could look like this:

THREE SESSIONS

	Swim	Bike	Run	Transition	Other
Mon	speed	skills			
Tue					
Wed	endurance				
Thu		speed			
Fri	speed				
Sat					
Sun		endurance			

FOUR SESSIONS

	Swim	Bike	Run	Transition	Other
Mon	speed				
Tue	endurance	speed			
Wed					
Thu	speed	speed			
Fri					
Sat	endurance	skills			
Sun		endurance			

FIVE SESSIONS					
	Swim	Bike	Run	Transition	Other
Mon	speed				
Tue	endurance	speed			
Wed	speed	skills			
Thu		speed			
Fri	endurance				
Sat	speed	endurance			
Sun		endurance			

EQUIPMENT

Of the three triathlon disciplines cycling has by far the greatest reliance on equipment. Although it is still the case that you are the most important element, the bike obviously plays a major part in transferring your skill, fitness and talent into results. A top-quality bike will not make a great rider better but a good bike will help any rider reach their potential. For a bicycle to perform well in a competitive environment and give you the confidence to perform to your best it must fit well and be mechanically sound. There are some components that will help you perform better and I will discuss these as we work through the mechanics of a bicycle below. You need to find a bike that fits and ensure that your bike is adjusted correctly to make you as efficient as possible.

You will find details on bikes designed specifically for women at the end of this section, along with a discussion on triathlon-specific bikes.

The bicycle

The bicycle is a phenomenally simple piece of design, although it is being continually refined and developed in every way possible.

The frame

The bicycle's main component is the frame. Frames have progressed hugely in the past few years. Twenty years ago every racing bike was made of steel tubing welded into place and then painted to the manufacturer's, customer's or sponsor's desire. Frames are now available in steel, aluminium, titanium, carbon fibre and any mixture of these. Frame materials offer different characteristics. A traditional steel frame will be longlasting, and will be comfortable because it will absorb shock from the road, but may be slightly

heavier than a comparable frame in carbon fibre while also being less stiff. Carbon fibre frames are stiff and light but can be uncomfortable and cannot be repaired once damaged. Aluminium frames are light but not as stiff as carbon fibre or in some instances steel frames. The extensive use of carbon fibre has introduced a much wider range of frame shapes and designs than was previously possible using metals. Compact frames, which look smaller and have sloping top tubes, have been introduced.

Frame size
As the frame is the heart of the bicycle it is vital that it is of the correct dimensions for you and is correctly set up. Using a frame that is too big or too small will have an impact on performance, handling and ultimately safety. While frame sizes always used to be given in seat-tube measurement but the length of the frame measured from seat-tube to *headset* or stem is also vitally important. Recent alterations in frame materials and sizing have made it more difficult than before to prescribe a frame size. With a more traditional frame design it was possible to work out the desired frame size from your inside leg measurement. Newer designs, along with an increase in the number of frames imported from different parts of the world – where measurements are taken from different parts of the frame – mean this calculation is no longer valid and your best bet may be to develop a relationship with a good local bicycle dealer or a good coach. There are also a number of bike-fitting services available. These are not cheap but can save you money in the long run and of course having an appropriately sized frame should enhance your performance. Compact framesets make measurement even harder, as while some of the older manufacturers provided over 60 different sizes, many compacts come in only three sizes.

Seat-post length/saddle setback
You will often see poorly fitted bikes where the owner has used the *saddle height* to compensate for an incorrectly sized frame or has used the seat rails to bring the saddle forward. This should be avoided as it has a detrimental effect on handling and therefore safety. See p. 90 for advice on positioning your saddle.

Handlebars
There are two types of handlebars used for competitive road cycling: the standard drop, or curly bar, and the more aerodynamic bullhorn or tri-bar combination. Drop handlebars allow the rider a wide variety of positions, reducing fatigue while allowing access to the brakes and gear-selection system. There is a great deal of variation even in drop handlebars, and whatever pair you select needs to be the correct size to ensure they are both comfortable and

TRAINING FOR THE USE OF TRI-BARS

Using tri-bars for the first time can be a bit daunting. To get used to the position practise either on the turbo trainer or in a traffic-free area. When you are on the tri-bars you don't have access to the brakes (though you may have access to the gear levers if on a time trial/triathlon specific bike). Get confident at riding at moderate speeds before trying to ride fast and at high levels of effort. Avoid trying to corner until you are extremely confident and only attempt very slight corners; even professional athletes come up off the bars to brake and corner in races.

safe. Drop handlebars should be the width of the shoulders of the rider. The other variables are depth, drop, reach and shape. A good bike shop will have a wide selection of bars. The importance of a handlebar with a shallower drop or reach is that people with shorter arms and smaller hands find these types of bars more comfortable. The shape of bars is more flexible nowadays as carbon fibre is more widely used, either exclusively or as a wrap over a metal. This allows flat sections in the bars and a squarer feel at the top of the bar. Some riders prefer this as it allows a greater range of positions, and getting a look at the different products available will help you find out what is best for you.

There are a wide variety of styles and designs for tri-bars but the basic principle of lowering the rider onto a pair of narrow bars and bringing the arms together to reduce height and frontal area remains consistent. It is possible to buy a pair of tribars to attach to standard bars. This is very popular as it is a great way of using one bike for both road racing and time trials. The clip-ons simply bolt on to the top of standard bars, providing a secondary position that is more aerodynamic and therefore faster. These bars come in a wide variety of lengths and are generally adjustable.

Handlebar stem

The handlebars are connected to the top of the frame forks by a stem. These stems come in a wide variety of designs and lengths. This component, when combined with spacers on top of the forks, can adjust the position of the handlebars significantly. There is a compromise to be made here between safety, comfort and performance. You are training for performance, but clearly safety should not be significantly compromised.

Braking systems

The components of the braking system are the brake lever, the brake cable and the brake caliper. The right-hand brake lever normally operates the front brake and the left-hand lever the rear brake. There is little variance in brake lever type and on standard road bikes the location of the lever can be adjusted slightly on the front curve of the bar to ensure that the lever can be reached and operated safely. Most road-bike levers also house the gear selector, and operating each individually may take a little getting used to. Some tri-bars have different types of levers though their method of operation is clearly the same. They are not adjustable in position but are easily accessible as they are generally located at the end of the base or bull-bar section of the handlebars. They are generally fitted into the end of the bars and are inverted to offer a good level of leverage.

The brake calipers work by having a number of parts that when pulled together squeeze the brake pads onto the rim of the wheel. The brake pads are a very important part of the system and must be in good order with plenty of material on them. Different rim types need different types of brake pad to operate well. Most wheels are aluminium and will work very well with the pads that are supplied as standard with the bike or calipers. If you are fortunate enough to have wheels that have carbon fibre as a braking surface you will also need specific brake pads designed to operate on this surface, failure to do this will result in excessive wear to the carbon fibre and impaired braking, especially when wet.

The cables should also receive attention as they transfer the action from the rider through the lever to the caliper so must be in good working order. They will need replacing every so often to ensure they remain an efficient part of the system. Cable systems these days are generally internally routed within the handlebars and often within the frame, this keeps them neat and out of the way of the weather. Ensure that when you transport your bike you don't create kinks in the cables and be aware of this if you make adjustments to the position of your handlebars or add tri-bars, as this can have a catastrophic impact on braking ability.

Chain set

Chain sets on road-race and time-trial bikes will normally have two *chainrings* though there is no reason why a rider can't race with a triple chain set, though there is obviously going to be a minor weight penalty. The chainrings are often described by their size with the smaller chainring generally having 39–42 teeth and the larger chainring having 49–54, with 52 being almost the industry standard. The size of the chainrings combined with the size of the rear sprockets and the circumference of the wheel makes the gear ratio. For example, a 52 by 13 refers to a gear that has a chainring size of 52 and a sprocket size of 13. The larger the difference between the chainring size and the sprocket size the larger the gear and therefore the further you will travel with every pedal revolution. A hilly race will require a wider range of gears than a flat event. Steep climbs will need smaller gears that are easier to push, such as a 39 by 22. Getting used to the gears that you have and the gears that you need to suit your abilities will take a little time, you can achieve this by experimenting during training.

There is some variance in chain set type other than number and size of chainrings. The material the chain set is made from will have an impact upon its weight and this is often a factor to consider when putting a bike together. There is some variance in the length of the cranks (the arms that attach the chainrings to the pedals), with some experienced riders preferring a longer crank to give them greater leverage. Generally the cranks supplied are 170 mm long and for the vast majority of riders and events this will be perfectly suitable. Experimenting with crank length is a fairly contentious subject and there are some parts of the sport where athletes attribute improvements in performance to crank lengths. Bear in mind that additional length will increase the angle that the knee is opened up at the top of the pedal stroke. This is not a good thing as it is at the point that the knee is about to be exposed to the greatest force. Given the risk it is worth noting that there is no substantive piece of evidence to suggest that there is any performance gain from altering crank lengths.

One of the other key changes in the past few years is the reintroduction of elliptical chainrings. Shimano introduced non-round rings in the 1980s with mixed success. These were discontinued but have been reintroduced by a number of other companies in the past five years. As yet there is no solid proof that these items have a great impact, but many professional cyclists use these rings, and manufacturers claim that they eliminate the dead spot at the top of the pedal stroke where the leg is not pushing or pulling the pedal around. This is not a cheap option but it is worth investigating if you are interested in the development of equipment.

Beyond this the selection of a chain set is probably going to be governed by budget and taste. There are aerodynamic-specific chain sets available and if you are pursuing the ultimate aerodynamic bike then you may wish to consider investing in such an item. Do bear in mind that you can spend a lot of money on gears, often without a significant gain in performance.

Gears

A racing bicycle will normally have a gear mechanism on the chain set called the front mech and on the rear sprockets called the rear mech. These are operated by cables from the gear levers, which are commonly found on the handlebars often within the brake lever. The gears move the chain across the sprockets and chainrings to vary the gear ratio available to the rider. Gear levers can also be found on the down tube (this was the norm until the late 1990s), and with time-trial bikes they can often be found at the end of the tri-bars. There are a number of manufacturers of gear systems, the selectors of which operate in subtly different ways. The major manufacturers are Shimano, SRAM and Campagnolo and each are used in equal measure by professional cyclists and amateurs alike. The choice is often very personal and can come down to aesthetics. Each manufacturer has a wide variety of component ranges, referred to as group sets, to enable a rider to meet their needs, preferences and budget. Campagnolo and Shimano also both manufacture electronic gear-changing systems. These are relatively new and are now being used extensively by professional cyclists, with systems filtering down to more affluent amateur cyclists. None of the systems available are cheap and there is some discussion about battery life and the ease of owner maintenance. It is a new concept to be investigated when considering equipment but it is likely to be quite some time before they become commonplace at amateur events.

The gear mechanisms themselves vary little between manufacturers though some material differences occur with an increased use of carbon fibre for both aesthetics and weight reduction. As with the braking system the cables must be in good state of repair and are crucial to the precise operation of the gear systems. They must be correctly adjusted to ensure the gear you want is selected and the mechanism shifts the chain and then keeps it in the correct place. Poor condition or maintenance can lead to sloppy changes or jumping between gears, both of which should be avoided. The number of sprockets on the rear cassette has steadily increased over the past 20 years, with most bikes now having 9, 10 or in the case of Campagnolo 11 sprockets on the rear cassette. This gives the rider a wide selection of gears and removes the need to select different sprockets for different kinds of racing. It is important to keep a close eye on the wear in the gear-changing and transmission systems. When gears start to slip (generally caused by worn cables or poorly adjusted gears) it can be potentially dangerous. It is not difficult to set up and maintain gears but if you are not confident then a regular service by a qualified bike mechanic will ensure that you stay safe and efficient. A consequence of increasing the number of sprockets (and therefore gears) available on a bike is that the width of the chain and the sprockets themselves has reduced. This has a negative impact on the lifespan of these parts, especially if they are used in wet weather.

Pedals

One of the advances in bicycle design in the past 25 years has been the introduction of *clipless pedals*. These pedals do not have the traditional toe clip that was common up until the late 1980s. The original clipless system was based upon the system used for skis, but there are now many clipless systems available. The systems are broadly similar with a fixing or cleat attached to the bottom of the cycling shoe that when pressed onto the pedal will click into place. Once in place the shoe will be securely fixed and only a small amount of movement will be possible until the rider wants to take the shoe off the pedal. A twist to the side will free the shoe from the

pedal. The one thing that is vital with all of these systems is the positioning of the cleat on the bottom of the shoe, which will then have a direct influence on the position of the foot over the pedal. It is vital the ball of your foot sits over the pedal axle and that the foot is in a neutral position. Sitting on a table and letting your feet dangle will show you the natural and neutral position of your feet. Take a note of this and then apply it to your pedal cleat as you fit it to your shoe. This measurement is probably less vital than it once was (because most pedal systems offer a degree of float to allow the foot to move

slightly when it is attached via the cleat to the pedal), but do not skimp on this setup as poorly fitted shoe plates can cause knee injuries. If you find you have painful knees after cycling, review your foot position and see if there is any wear on one side of the shoe plate as this may indicate the direction in which it should be adjusted. It is worth keeping an eye on wear on the shoe plates, as they don't last forever and a worn shoe plate can also lead to painful knees. Advice on suitability for any specific rider is best given by your local independent bicycle dealer.

Wheels

There are a huge number of different wheels available to the racing cyclist, and many entry-level racing bikes are supplied with good-quality wheels. A long time ago all racing wheels were hand-built by highly skilled and experienced wheel builders who would use the hub and rim of your choice, lacing them with high-quality spokes. This practice has been altered significantly by the introduction of high-quality, very durable and light machine-built wheels. Many spokes are now flattened to be more aerodynamic and the method of lacing has also changed. Rim technology has also moved on, with carbon fibre being used in preference to aluminium to produce lighter, more aerodynamic wheels, often with deeper rims. These wheels are great for time trialling and can be used in road racing but are more susceptible to side winds and can be difficult to handle in a group situation when it is breezy. Selection of wheels is again very personal with aesthetics and budget being important factors. You will see a wide variety of wheel designs at most races and a quick chat with different users will give you an idea of the advantages and disadvantages of differing designs. The type of racing you will be doing should also be considered when you are selecting a wheel set. Also if you are using one pair of wheels for training and racing you may select something that is slightly more hard-wearing and robust, which is also easy to maintain and repair. Deep-rimmed carbon-fibre wheels are now used extensively in racing and the weight of these wheels can be very low. If you are physically small you may be blown about by these wheels and a lighter pair of wheels with a smaller rim side section will be more suitable. If you are racing or riding in mountainous terrain you may also consider using different wheels as deeper rims may not be suitable for long mountain descents. The other key consideration for wheels is the type of tyres that the wheels take. This will generally have a greater influence on the handling of the bike than the selection of the wheels. There are three types of tyre system.

- **Tubular tyres:** Also referred to as sew-ups because the inner tube is sewn inside the casing before the tyre is glued to the rim of the wheel. This type of wheel was until fairly recently the only type of wheel used for racing. There are many riders who still use this system and it has the advantage that the tyres can be run at higher pressures, which can make them faster. If they puncture they generally stay on the rim keeping things safer. You are not allowed assistance in triathlon, and tubular tyres are easy to change quickly should you be unfortunate enough to have a puncture during competition. This type of tyre also suffers less from pinch punctures than the high-pressure system. On the downside tubular tyres are expensive and very difficult to repair.

- **HP (high pressure) tyres:** This system is made up of a tyre that is wired to a rim with an inner tube inside it, and is the type of tyre that most people will be familiar with. This system is easy to operate and maintain as it is generally very robust. There is huge variety of tyre available and everyone will have their own preference based upon performance, experience and even colour. Inner tubes are relatively cheap and easy to replace and it is easy to keep a spare with you when out training. This type of tyre is by far the best option for training purposes.
- **Tubeless tyres:** A relatively new arrival, and similar in appearance to the HP tyre, this system seals a tyre on a rim with a valve so pressure can be maintained. The downside is that there is a narrow choice of rims available and a narrow choice of tyres available. Repairing punctures while out on the road can also be difficult. These tyres suffer fewer pinch punctures and can be very responsive, but are less suitable to triathlon than other types.

Whatever you select, your wheels need to be well maintained. Check that the wheels spin freely and quietly and are true and round. This is important for safety as a buckled wheel will have impaired braking performance. Probably the single most important factor is the quality of the outer cover of the tyre and the pressure at which it is run. Tyres should be free of rips and tears and should have sufficient tread on them. Tyre pressure needs to be correct for both safety and performance. The appropriate pressure is printed on the side of the tyre and it is worth checking before every ride (and certainly before your race).

Bicycle setup

Now that you understand the components of a bicycle you can take a closer look at establishing the correct position for a rider. The three areas that need to be considered are safety, comfort and efficiency. As you are concentrating on cycling for sport, efficiency is the most important. This does not mean that safety and comfort will be ignored but there will be some minor compromises to achieve an efficient and fast position. This is probably best demonstrated by the position adopted for time trialling, where the rider is in such a position that they cannot easily access the brake levers or indeed change position without significant body movement. The traditional road-race position is probably less of a compromise but it is still less comfortable and safe than the position found on a non-racing bike.

Contact points

When working on cycle position you need to look at the points of contact, comprised of the pedals, the saddle and the handlebars.

Contact points and variable body position

This diagram shows that altering the position of any one of these contact points has an impact upon performance, as this critical triangle has a substantial influence on how you transfer power to the bike. If you are very new to cycling then your position (represented by the angle between straight leg and body) may be more relaxed. You may seek to develop your aerodynamics as your confidence in bike-handling also improves. You can do this by working on your leg and core flexibility and by gradually altering your position on the bike. This can achieve great positional and performance improvements but changes have to be made very slowly so that injuries are not sustained. Again I will look at the positioning for triathlon-specific and time-trial bikes in more detail shortly.

As the principal point of power transfer the pedal is arguably the most important point of contact with the bike. Much of the setup in this area will refer to the adjustment of the cleat on the bottom of the shoe. First of all you need to use cycling shoes that fit you well. Providing this is the case the cleat needs to be set up to ensure that the ball of the foot is directly over the axle of the pedal. This position will ensure that power will flow through the pedal as efficiently as possible. This position will also help prevent injuries to the knee, which can be caused by poorly adjusted cleats. Once in place the foot should feel comfortable without any tension on the knee. If you feel your knee being twisted then alter the cleat very slightly. Adjustments in this area only need to be very small, and you may need to use a bit of trial and error to establish the right position for you, though the basic principle of ball of foot over axle will give you the starting point for an effective position.

Next concentrate on the height of the saddle. Measure from the top of the pedal axle to the top of the saddle. This allows for variance in saddle type, giving you a measure that can be applied to any bicycle you may ride.

The basic formula for establishing the distance from the pedal axle to the top of the saddle is:

Inseam × 1.09 (⁺/₋ 0.3 i.e. 1.06 – 1.12)

Apply this to an inseam of 82 cm

$$82 \times 1.06 = 86.92$$
$$82 \times 1.09 = 89.38$$
$$82 \times 1.12 = 91.84$$

This gives a range and I would suggest starting with the centre figure and setting this as the saddle height. Once you have done this try the bike for size wearing your cycling shorts and your cycling shoes. Once in place, your leg should be almost but not entirely straight.

If you have been riding extensively prior to carrying out these measurements than any adjustment that you make should be minor and if any large adjustment should be made gradually – certainly no more than 5 mm per week.

Once you have established the correct position for the height of the saddle you will need to look at the lateral adjustment and the tilt of the saddle. With saddle tilt it is best to start the process with a saddle that is effectively flat. This can then be adjusted to find a more comfortable position. Many women find a downwards tilt more comfortable but this should only be slight and experimentation is the key to getting a comfortable long-term setup.

The lateral adjustment of the saddle is a little more prescriptive as this has a direct impact on the efficiency of the pedalling action. The saddle should be laterally adjusted so that when normally seated and with the pedal in the '3 o'clock' position the rider's knee is almost over the pedal axle. If substantial adjustment of the lateral position of the saddle is required to achieve this, a further check of the saddle height must be completed to ensure this measurement is still accurate and relevant.

The handlebars should be in such a position that the rider can reach the brake levers safely while not being too upright (as this is not aerodynamic). This can be achieved by altering the height of the handlebars by inserting or removing spacers at the top of the handlebars and by changing the length of the stem.

Adjusting the position of the handlebars will not compensate for a frame that is either too large or too small and may result in a bike that is dangerous to ride due to unpredictable handling.

Setting up tri-bars is an added complication and here the main objective is to get low and reduce frontal area though the position should not be compromised as power output and subsequently speed will suffer. Therefore, once you have established the correct position for the saddle regarding height and lateral movement the handlebars should be set up to achieve the aerodynamic, low position. Remember the diagram on p. 89, which shows the relationship between the position of the body and the handlebars.

A good position will maintain your efficiency and improve your drag. Many riders move further forward on the saddle to achieve low positions at the front, and some riders even move the saddle forward to enable a low back and an aerodynamic position. This can, if taken too far, reduce power output. There is a school of thought that reductions in power can be compensated for by increased aerodynamics and reduced drag. This may be the case, up to a point, in a wind tunnel, but on the road the situation is less exact and there is a huge danger that this philosophy will slow you down. Unless you have access to a power measurement device you are unlikely to be able to constantly test your positions. Keeping your aerodynamic position close to your standard road position, in the critical phase of saddle and pedal interaction, will ensure that all the training you will be doing in this position is not impaired by racing in a substantially different position. You will need to practise your aerodynamic position if you plan to use one, so as you approach race day spend at least one or two sessions a week on your time-trial bike.

If you do have access to a power meter then use your turbo trainer to assess your aerodynamic positions. Ensure you use a set of controlled conditions and a standard warm-up as in our other tests, then ride at a specific heart rate and speed and check your power output over a period of 10 minutes. This will show if there are any substantial differences in power in the aerodynamic position.

Racing bikes for women

On average, relative to overall height, women have longer legs and shorter torsos than men because the thigh bone tends to make up a higher percentage of leg length in women. This is especially true in taller women, who make up a high percentage of the *elite* triathlete and cycling population. Women also tend to be on average shorter than men. Most importantly, women tend to have narrower shoulders and smaller feet and hands.

What does this mean for bike design and setup? Traditionally bikes were sized simply according to inside leg length or 'stand-over height' (and, sadly, in many shops they still are). However, for most women this will lead to too big a frame given their proportionally longer legs relative to height. This may result in you being sold a short stem and an in-line seat pin to shorten the distance from saddle to handlebars. This is a highly unsatisfactory compromise. The handling of the bike will be deleteriously affected and the position of the knees relative to the feet (too far forward) will cause poor power transfer and, probably, sore knees. All in all, an uncomfortable and unresponsive ride.

Current recommendations for sizing bicycles are more focused on top-tube length so many women are simply sold a smaller frame size in order to get the correct top-tube length. But this in itself is only half the problem. Stem length and saddle position still need to be optimised. Also, there may not always be a smaller sized frame available.

There are an increasing number of cycle manufacturers looking to cash in on the expansion in the marketplace by offering female-specific road bikes and other equipment. 'Women's Specific Geometry' is promoted as, in the main, a shorter top-tube and smaller frame sizes. While the latter is undoubtedly very helpful the former may or may not be the answer: it depends on how this is achieved.

The simplest, and therefore cheapest, way to achieve a shorter bike top-tube is to bring the seat-tube forward to bring the saddle closer to the handlebars. In practice this usually means making the seat-tube more upright, i.e. steeper.

In order for maximal transmission of power from the contraction of the powerful thigh muscles to the pedals the foot and knee must be properly aligned over the pedal spindle. Sitting too far forward or back will result in inefficient power transmission and possibly knee pain.

To achieve an optimal knee/foot/pedal position a female rider will need to sit well behind the *bottom-bracket* area. In those designs where the top-tube is created by steepening the seat-tube the opposite happens. So, our rider moves the saddle as far back as it will go. The reach is now again too long so she buys a shorter handlebar stem and she is back to square one.

The best way to achieve a truly female-specific frame is to redesign the whole geometry of the bicycle to give a shorter top-tube and a shallower seat-tube angle. The leaders in this field have to be American Bicycle Group: the designers and manufacturers of Quintano Roo, Merlin and Litespeed. They have not only invested in a full geometrical redesign for their frames but also for a range of forks which give excellent race-bike-handling qualities even on smaller bikes.

Components and accessories for female cyclists

There are lots on the market – but which of these do you really need? Yes, narrower bars will help optimise the riding position, making it more aerodynamic (smaller frontal area) and will also take some of the strain off the shoulders, but these bars also need to be shorter front to back. Shimano Ultegra shifter levers are available with an inset wedge to fit smaller hands, and the new Dura Ace ones are shaped so that the risk of accidentally putting on the brakes while shifting gear is minimised. However, in general Campagnolo levers offer a better grip for smaller hands and are easier to operate from the brake hoods. Most women seem to prefer riding on the brake hoods to drop-bar bends. This has often been assumed to be due to shorter reach (of the raised handlebar issue) but is undoubtedly due to smaller hands feeling more secure while braking from this position compared with fingertip-only contact drop handlebars. Crank and stem length need to be proportional to the bike and the rider not used as a way of adapting the bike to fit. A smaller woman with small feet will benefit from shorter cranks – not for ease of spinning, the lighter muscles will aid that anyway, but simply to make the bike fit her.

Saddles

Women don't necessarily require wider saddles – in fact most women's hip measurement is smaller than most men's. In truth, when riding in a forward-leaning race position the weight is borne not by the pelvic bones but further forward. This is more so in women than in men due to forward rotation of the pelvis. Therefore the ideal women's racing saddle should be long and not too wide at the back, so you can move backwards to get power from your thighs; and soft and slightly tilted down at the front to alleviate pressure.

Triathlon-specific bikes

There are triathlon-specific bikes available and over the years there has been a great deal of marketing aimed at this section of the cycling community. If you are inexperienced then there probably isn't a huge gain in riding a triathlon-specific bike as opposed to a good-quality road bike. As you progress you may develop your bike and equipment to suit you and your type of racing. In the elite form of triathlon the bikes used are the same as road-race bikes, some riders use smaller tri-bars on the bikes but broadly speaking this is the only adaptation. The use of tri-bars on road bikes is one of the more common adaptations that triathletes make to bikes.

The next natural progression from here is the full time-trial or triathlon bike. This is a machine developed to be aerodynamic and have time-trial handlebars built on to it. Using a bike like this if you don't have flexibility or experience can be a little scary as the positions you have to adopt can be quite extreme. Handling can sometimes be very different to a road bike and as such if you do decide to go in this direction you must be sure that you have lots of time to practice before race day to make sure you are competent and confident on a machine of this type. Cycling and triathlon magazines are full of shiny new bits of equipment that don't offer any guarantees and often cost a great deal of money. While it is entirely up to you where you spend your hard-earned cash don't lose sight of the fact that it is the engine that powers the bike (i.e. you) that is the most important factor. Focus on making sure you are the fittest and fastest rider you can be. There have been many athletes over the years that have spent thousands of pounds on expensive equipment to make the bike faster when they could have had the same performance impact by training a bit harder or shedding a little more weight. Having said this, a nice bike that is a pleasure to ride, train and race on is a huge motivating factor, just make sure you keep your eye on the goal when considering equipment and don't let the flashy adverts and shiny components sway you too much.

Clothing

Training throughout the year is going to be important to enable you to achieve your goals and therefore the right clothing is vitally important.

Shorts and legwear

Probably the single most important piece of clothing to enhance comfort and therefore performance is a pair of cycling shorts. These shorts are cut specifically to make cycling comfortable and will be higher in the back to keep this area warm and covered when you are leaning forward. They will have flat seams to prevent rubbing and chafing and they will have a degree of padding in the saddle area. There are some shorts specifically designed for women and shorts come in a wide variety of sizes colours and designs. Generally speaking the more you pay the better quality the shorts will be but this does not mean that an inexpensive pair will not be serviceable and comfortable. Shorts also come with what is referred to as a bib. Bib shorts are preferred by many cyclists as there is no waistband, which many riders feel constricting. The downside of these shorts is that they are difficult to get off when the call of nature is pressing. The insert in any pair of shorts is very important and must stay clean; you need to keep a close eye on them to ensure they are not snagged or creased as this can cause pressure points. Finally the way in which the ends of shorts hold on the legs is important. Generally, shorts will have some form of elastic to hold the short legs in place. This stops them riding up and bunching, which causes sores. You will need to see what suits you best as there are different types of leg grips some of which can be quite tight.

Initially running leggings can be used on top of cycling shorts for cooler days though they must be close-fitting around the ankle to prevent any obstruction of the moving parts of the bicycle. There are plenty of specifically designed cycling leggings and tights, and these will generally be very close-fitting and made from a material that will dry quickly and retain some protection even when wet. To keep your legs warm when training in colder weather you will use either a cycling-specific legging or leg-warmers. These leggings are cut specifically for cycling and, much like cycling shorts, have either a waist or a bib. Leg-warmers are held in place by putting them under the leg of the shorts, which makes them very useful as they can be removed mid-ride if the weather warms up. They can also be purchased in a variety of lengths from full leg to knees only. This gives even more flexibility for training.

T-shirts and jerseys
Your upper body needs to be kept warm and make you as visible to other road users as possible. There are many types of cycling jerseys in a massive array of designs.

Cycling jerseys are important as they provide good coverage to the lower back, zip up around the neck, are specifically cut for cycling and have storage in the right places. What is probably more important is that you have appropriate clothing to keep you warm and safe if you have a fall. The best way of achieving this is to use layers whenever you are riding. This could simply be a base layer under a cycling top in the summer through to multiple warm layers under a jacket in the winter. It is generally accepted that it is a good idea to have a base layer on regardless of the weather as a safety measure; materials sliding over each other can shield you from contact with the road if you fall off your bike. Any base layer that you wear should be of a technical material. This means one that is designed for exercise and doesn't absorb sweat, keeping the rider cooler, warmer and drier. Tops of this type come in a variety of thicknesses and with long, short and no sleeves. Adding an outside

jacket for warmth and protection from the rain should give you a complete set of cycling clothing that will enable you to train in all weathers. Outer jackets can be expensive but should be water-resistant, warm and breathable. This one garment will make cycling through the British winter possible and even pleasurable.

Gloves

Gloves are important both for warmth and for protection in the case of an accident. Cold hands have little control over brakes and gears, and your hands will almost always be extended in the event of a crash or fall. The fit of a glove is important and paying close attention to the conditions you intend to ride in will help you stay at the right temperature; full-fingered gloves will obviously give more protection from the cold than short-fingered track mitts. There are gloves suitable for cycling in sub-zero temperatures and if you intend to get out in the coldest weather or if you suffer from cold hands these gloves may be worth the investment though they can be very expensive. There are multiple-layer systems, which offer flexibility and durability while giving great protection from the cold; these are also expensive, but a good option. You will probably need several pairs of gloves to cover the entire year from very cold winter mornings through to chilly spring mornings and mitts for the summer.

Helmets

While not a legal requirement for riding on the road, using a helmet is just common sense. A cycle helmet should carry a CE mark and an assurance that it meets European Standard EN1078. This will be found on a small label or sticker inside the helmet. Once you have established that the helmet is the correct type then the fitting must be considered. A helmet must sit on the head with the chinstrap snugly underneath the chin to prevent excessive movement while riding or in the event of an accident. Helmets come in a huge variety of designs and trying out several helmets will give you a feel for what's available. The method by which the helmet fits itself onto the head is vital as differing systems suit different people's head shapes and sizes. Ventilation design of your helmet is also very important, and huge advances have been made in the past 10 years.

Also available are aerodynamic helmets for racing. These have evolved over the past 10 years from what were simple head fairings, designed to improve aerodynamics but not necessarily providing protection, through to full safety helmets that offer considerable aerodynamic advantages. There are a huge number of aerodynamic helmets on the market but there are some considerations if you would like to use one of these for racing. Many of these helmets are designed for cycle time trials and as such may not be the fastest items to take on and off. This is of course a significant issue in a triathlon; you won't want to waste time putting it on and taking it off. The very design means they are often fully enclosed, so if you are planning a long-distance race or a race in a very warm part of the world this may be a significant factor in your overall performance. Many aerodynamic helmets are fitted with visors; these can be helpful but you may find them uncomfortable. Whichever helmet you choose you need to practise in it and get used to taking it on and off.

Footwear

Footwear can have a significant effect on performance for the triathlete. Cycling shoes allow a much greater transfer of power to the pedals and facilitate a much more accurate positioning of the foot than trainers. Whatever footwear is used it should be securely fastened and of the correct size. There are a number of different methods of attaching the foot to the pedal, traditionally toe-clips and straps were attached to the pedals and provided a method of securing the foot and aiding the transfer of power. The majority of cyclists now use a clipless pedal (see above). There are as many designs of cycling shoe as there are types of trainers and finding the right one for you by trial and error will prove costly. Find a good local cycling shop that stocks at least two brands of shoe so you can try them out. When you do settle on a brand consider the fastening system as you will need to put this shoe on during Transition 1. Make sure you avoid shoes with ratchet systems unless you are doing long-distance races where the additional security that these system offer may be worth the extra time they take to fasten.

Static trainers

There is a very wide range of turbo trainers available now, as well as spinning and exercise bikes. The turbo trainer has the significant advantage of offering training effect on your own bike, making it closer to a real-life race situation. There are a number of exercise and spinning bikes now available that claim to do the same thing. These can be very expensive so make sure that you try before you buy and get something that replicates both the position you ride in and feels similar to the feel of your bike on the road.

Static trainers can allow you to run fitness-specific training sessions and carry out some technique work that may not be possible on the road. They are also useful for training when the weather makes it unsafe to train outside (e.g. in snow, ice or wind) or when it is dark and time is restricted. Training with an indoor trainer is most effective when using interval (rather than skills or endurance) training methods, as you can train in very short intense bursts in a way that would be unsafe on the open road.

The one aspect of skills training that can be done effectively on a turbo trainer is pedalling. Developing a swift, fluid and controlled pedalling style can be done on the turbo and is best undertaken in a light and easy gear pedalling at between 90–100 rpm. You can even extend this and do some single leg drills to help you improve your pedalling technique. You can do 1 minute per leg and then 1 minute on both and repeat this number of times. This can make a very effective, and not too boring, recovery session that enables you to practise cycling skills after a tough session out on the bike. You will quickly realise that one leg is stronger and more technically able than the other and you can target this by working one leg at a time.

Many turbo trainers have variable resistance. This is not essential but can be useful. There are various ways the different types of trainer add resistance, from the use of wind (hence the name turbo trainer), to magnets and/or fluids, the major differences being the noise and vibration that they create. This may not be an issue if you use it in your garage at home but if you live in an upstairs flat it may be a significant factor as the noise and vibration from a fan trainer can be considerable when compared to a smooth fluid trainer or good-quality magnetic trainer.

You can get specific tyres for your turbo trainer and if you plan to do the bulk of your winter preparation on one then this may be a worthwhile investment. If you are using the turbo trainer infrequently then it may not be worth worrying about, just keep an eye on the wear of the tyre. It is worth using a towel or other protective material to keep sweat off your bike and you will also need to keep another towel handy to dry yourself as you train.

04

RUNNING

TECHNIQUE TRAINING

Running is the final part of the event, and in many ways this can make it the most important. Tactically you may have held back in the other two disciplines to save some energy and effort for the run. If this is the case you need to leave nothing behind on the run and give it your all. Even if your strategy is just to hold a good steady effort throughout the event and across the disciplines then the run is still the last section of the race and as such should have the remainder of your energy devoted to it. Runners have differing techniques; some of which are more efficient than others. Techniques are governed, to a certain extent, by limb length, body shape and fitness levels. There is a limit to how much a running style can be changed but improvements are always possible. The basic principle of endurance running is: *speed = stride length × stride frequency*. This is a very simple concept but many people overlook it. Stride length is the distance that you cover from one step to the next. Stride frequency is a lot like cadence on a bike (see p. 155) and can be measured in steps per minute. These two variables form the basis of how you run and the elements you can control to make you run faster.

The basics of a good running technique are as follows:

- **Head**: should be still with little up and down movement, look forward and keep as relaxed as possible.
- **Arms**: bent at the elbow to approximately 90 degrees, relaxed. Movement should be forward as well as across the body, and should be small, controlled and efficient. Do not hold the hands in fists, keep the grip loose as if you are holding something fragile between your first finger and thumb.
- **Trunk**: erect, relaxed, hips forward. Keep the body stable as if it is being held still with other limbs moving around it.
- **Shoulders**: relaxed, loose and flexible. Pushed neither back nor forward.
- **Foot-strike**: under body, either in mid-sole, side of foot or heel. Foot should be pointing forward.
- **Take off**: push off quickly after foot-strike, heel should come up towards the buttocks.
- **Stride length**: comfortable and in proportion to body.
- **Stride frequency**: optimum is around 180 strides per minute (90 strikes per foot per minute).

Looking in more detail at running technique, the leg action can be split into a number of phases.

The front support phase

The objective of this phase is to minimise deceleration of the body across the ground as the foot strikes the floor. With each strike the foot contacts the ground on the part of the foot that is most natural for the athlete, this may be the ball of the foot but may also be the whole foot depending on the style of the runner. A strike by the heel is to be avoided as this will lead to a decelerating force moving up the body from the foot. The leg cushions the ground-contact in a controlled way to minimise braking forces. Arm action is similar to sprinting but less active or pronounced.

The drive phase

The objective of this phase is to optimise forward motion. The athlete's weight rolls over the foot and off the toe of the shoe. Hips, knees and ankle joints extend during this phase; however, in longer distance races this extension may not be complete, and you need to ensure that the motion it creates is slightly upwards but predominantly forward. The feeling should be one of pushing and extending. This is the part of the technique concerned with power.

The recovery phase

The objective of this phase is to contribute to an efficient action and rhythm. This phase begins with the foot breaking contact with the ground, with the trailing leg flexing at the knee and then moving up towards the backside. The height the heel is brought towards the backside, and the degree of flexion at the knee is dependent on running speed. This is more pronounced in sprinting activities and less pronounced at slower running speeds.

The forward swinging phase

The objective of this phase of the leg cycle is to prepare for an active foot-strike. The recovery leg swings through past the body and upward, in a manner less pronounced than in sprinting. Generally, the slower the speed the lower the knee lift. Once the leg has passed to the front of the body, with the hip flexed, the leg will lower and the knee will extend. The foot then moves down and back relative to the body in preparation to minimise braking at foot-strike.

As a general guideline, your body should always be over the lead foot as it strikes the ground. If this is not the case your stride length is too long and the foot striking ahead of the body will apply a braking force prior to the body passing over the foot, thus slowing you down. Ideally the foot-plant should be in a straight line in the direction of travel, to ensure that the forces at the take-off phase are propelling you forward. Do not worry if you are displaying other characteristics such as splay footing or pigeon toeing unless this is creating injury issues. If you suspect that this is the case, then you should seek out the attention of a physiotherapist to correct the fault.

Drills

Drills are widely referred to in both run and swim coaching sessions and are designed to develop running action. A drill is simply a specific practice that is used to emphasise and improve a component of technique. They act by isolating and concentrating on only one aspect of the running action. Many triathlons are won and lost on the run sections of the course – not through lack of stamina, but through an inability to employ an efficient running style. Some basic running drills are listed opposite.

New drills are regularly developed and through spending time working with a number of coaches, you will develop additional drills that can be applied to your sessions. When designing drills you need to consider what aspect of technique you want to improve, as well as the technique of actually conducting the drill itself.

When using drills to improve technique you should ensure that you are not tired beforehand. Drills should therefore be included at the start of the session, after the warm-up. Drills should be carried out over a short distance (25–50 m) with a walk back to facilitate recovery and should be repeated between three and six times. When the main body of training is introduced after the drills, you should keep in mind the purpose of the drills and focus on this during the next component of the session.

Drills can also be very beneficial in acting as a recovery session. This is because they move the limbs through a greater range of motion, thus maintaining the range of movement and dynamic flexibility. Drills can also be used in the warm-up phase. If doing so, take care to ensure that you are fully warm before doing the drill as the drills extend the limbs outside the normal range of motion.

Distance training

The overall aim is to complete the race distance at a comfortable pace, subsequently building confidence. Distance training will also serve to increase running efficiency and aerobic endurance. When planning these sessions initially, the terrain should be flat and unchallenging, as the distance covered will represent the main challenge. Because these will be long training sessions, you need to think about the running surface. Grass, off-road and tartan (i.e. the traditional spongy-surface used for professional events) running tracks are a much better alternative to asphalt roads and pavements, and will greatly reduce impact to the legs. As you improve in fitness, ability and confidence, the use of hilly courses can be used to add to the intensity of the session. Initially for novices it may be more useful to work on time rather than distance, for example: run for a set period 5, 10, 20 or 30 minutes and rest for a set period, of between 30 seconds and 3 minutes, depending on how you feel.

BASIC DRILLS		
Drill	**Technique**	**Purpose**
High knees	Short, very fast steps lifting knees high in front of the body.	Improves running cadence (also known as stride frequency). Improves recovery phase of trail leg. Improves range of motion from the hip.
Kickbacks	With hands on bottom, kick feet back to touch the hands using a fast action.	Improves running cadence. Improves recovery of trail leg. Improves stride length.
Arm drives	Same as high knees but focus on driving arms through and pumping.	Improves upper body alignment. Improves co-ordination and arm balance.
Hills	15–30-sec uphill running on a steepish slope.	Improves stride length. Improves push-off.
Striding arm drive	Focus on arm action, all movement driving forward focus on keeping head still.	Reduces excess movement.
Downhill running	Lean slightly forward, 'float', avoid braking.	Improves leg cadence. Improves stride length.
Long rear legs	Make singular effort to push ground away. Leave foot in contact with ground a fraction longer than normal.	Improves the recovery phase of the cycle.

The distances covered can be up to twice race-distance for sprint- and standard-distance triathlon and 75–100 per cent of race-distance for long-distance athletes. This type of training should be emphasised during the early half of the training programme if you are planning on increasing your pace. If you do not have a target time, and your goal is simply to complete the event, distance training could make up your entire schedule.

Interval training

The use of interval training has been discussed in both the swimming and cycling chapters and the same DIRT principles can be applied to running. As further progression is applied, the athletes can be charged with either:

- reducing the rest periods;
- increasing the intensity of the work periods (running faster/harder);
- increasing the distance, along with the length of rest periods.

Do not try to change all three variables at once, as this could lead to injury and overtraining.

INTERVAL TRAINING SESSION EXAMPLES

It is important to plan each individual session to get the most out of it. An example of a complete session involving skills work is given below.

SKILLS SESSION EXAMPLE			
Day	Monday	**Discipline**	Cycling
Time	6.00 p.m.	**Location**	Falls Park outer circuit
Warm-up	Gentle jog 15 min steady.		
Main body	High-knee drill for 200 m, 1000 m steady jog and repeat 5 times. Heel-kick drill for 200 m, 100 m steady jog and repeat 5 times.		
Cool down	Reversal of warm-up.		
Stretching	At home, stretch legs and back		
Comment			

SPEED SESSION EXAMPLE			
Day	Wednesday	**Discipline**	Cycling
Time	6.00 p.m.	**Location**	Falls Park outer circuit
Warm-up	20-min run increasing pace and effort during the last 5 min		
Main body	500 m as hard as can hold, 1500 m steady, repeat six times.		
Cool down	Steady jog for 10 min		
Stretching	At home, stretch legs and back.		
Comment			

SPRINT SESSION EXAMPLE			
Day	Wednesday	**Discipline**	Cycling
Time	6.00 p.m.	**Location**	Central stadium track
Warm-up	15 laps steady warm-up increasing in final 5 min.		
Main body	Sprint final 50 m of every second lap. Repeat 10 times. Then reduce to every lap for 5 laps until you do a lap with no sprint. Then sprint each 50 m straight (2 per lap) for 10 laps.		
Cool down	10 min jogging		
Stretching	At home, stretch legs, arms and back.		
Comment			

HEART-RATE ZONES

As with cycling, one of the ways to measure the training intensity of your running is to use a heart-rate monitor. The best way to do so for running is to use heart-rate reserve.

Many runners calculate their heart rate training zones as a percentage of their max HR. Basing training zones on a percentage of your heart-rate reserve (HRR) is a fairly accurate way of prescribing training intensities because it takes into account both your max HR and your resting heart rate. Your HRR is simply your max HR minus your resting heart rate, and reflects how much your heart rate can increase to provide more oxygen to your muscles.

To calculate your HRR, you need to know your resting heart rate. The best way to determine your resting heart rate is to wear a heart-rate monitor to bed and check your heart rate as soon as you wake up. Do this for several days,

HEART-RATE TRAINING ZONES FOR RUNNING

Heart-rate zone 1	60–70% maximum heart rate	Long, slow runs, easy or recovery runs.	Training in this zone will improve your heart's ability to pump blood and your muscles' ability to utilise oxygen. Your body will become more efficient at feeding the working muscles, and will start to use fat as a source of fuel.
Heart-rate zone 2	70–80%	Aerobic, or target heart rate, zone.	Most effective for overall cardiovascular fitness. Increases your ability to transport oxygenated blood to muscle cells and carbon dioxide away from these cells. Also effective for increasing overall muscle strength.
Heart-rate zone 3	80–90%	Anaerobic zone.	The lactate threshold, i.e. the point at which the body cannot remove lactic acid as quickly as it is produced. Training in this zone helps to increase your lactate threshold, thus improving performance. Training in this zone will feel difficult: you will breathe heavily and your muscles will become tired.
Heart-rate zone 4	90–100%	VO_2max/ red line zone.	Only train in this zone if you're very fit, and only for very short periods of time. Lactic acid develops quickly as you are operating in oxygen debt to the muscles Training in this zone will increase fast-twitch muscle fibres and therefore speed.

and use the lowest rate as your resting heart rate. If you wake to an alarm, your heart rate may be elevated, so check your resting heart rate when you are able to wake naturally.

Establishing your maximal heart rate can be done either through experience gathered in races or very hard training.

Once you know your resting heart rate and max HR, calculating training zones based on HRR is easy.

EQUIPMENT

You can run in most types of clothing but if you are to training seriously throughout the year you will benefit from some specific running apparel to make training more enjoyable and comfortable. There are items that you can transfer from your cycling wardrobe but there are also running-specific items that are cut differently and which won't be appropriate on the bike. The same applies in the other direction.

Shoes

It is vital that you get a running shoe that is right for you, and the best way of doing this is to visit a specialist running retailer. If you have an old pair of shoes, take these with you so that the retailer can see how your shoes have worn. This will give them an indication of your running style, which in turn will help them to identify the best shoe for you. If you can afford it then buy two pairs. This will mean you can swap pairs between runs and help reduce overall

wear by giving the shoes time to recover between sessions. Be clear to the shop staff what you are training for, how much training you have done and what your targets are. As you approach race day you can always return to buy some race-specific shoes. Again be guided by the experts in the shop and ask for, and take, advice.

Socks

Socks are the next important thing to consider. If socks are comfortable then you won't even notice them, but if they are not they can cause a great deal of issues and disrupt your training programme. You should try some running-specific socks in the early session of your programme. You are likely to run without socks during your race, as it is very tricky and time-consuming to get socks on during a transition zone. Running without socks is something you need to build up to. Using talcum powder inside the shoe will help both in terms of getting the shoe on and preventing the shoe from rubbing. Clearly you will need to practise this and get used to it beforehand, so this is something to add to one of the training sessions as you progress.

Legwear

While your legs will keep themselves warm, the joints will be working hard and need to be looked after. Running trousers are normally very close-fitting to avoid bunching and chafing. A firm but not too tight waistband is also important, as is fitting around the calf to prevent flapping and trip hazards. There are lots of leggings of this kind on the market. Find a design you like while considering visibility to other road users, especially if you are running during twilight or darkness (this may well be inevitable as you train through the winter). As the weather gets warmer you will need shorts. Again running-specific shorts will be much more comfortable and come in two basic styles – the traditional short athletic-style running shorts, or the more close-fitting shorts that look a lot like cycling shorts but lack the padding. These shorts are relatively cheap and you will need to experiment a little to find what suits you best. On race day you are probably going to be wearing a *trisuit*, which is generally a one-piece suit similar to a woman's swimsuit, though often with longer leg sections. These leg sections are similar to the close-fitting style of running shorts so it will be worth getting used to running in these.

Tops

The upper part of the body is a little more flexible. For cycling, clothing layers are key and this remains true of running, though you are likely to need fewer layers as you will generate more and lose less heat because your speed through the air will be a lot lower and wind-chill will be less. Technical fabrics close to the skin will help wick sweat away from the body which will in turn help temperature regulation and prevent t-shirts from rubbing and causing sores. You can layer up on top of the base layer, bearing in mind that it is always advantageous to use technical fabrics. On the outside you could wear a light waterproof layer in wet or windy conditions. This can make you overly warm but can help make training throughout the year possible. Visibility is also always a safety issue so bright or florescent clothing is the most appropriate.

Accessories

Gloves are used by lots of runners in cold weather. They should be lightweight wherever possible. You may also want a hat when it's cold (or very hot). Glasses can improve visibility and protect you from flies.

TRANSITION AND GENERAL TRAINING

TRANSITION

Triathlon is unique in its structure, and the transition element (simply put the transferring from one discipline to the next) requires technical expertise that won't have been learned from other sports. For novices to triathlon, the transition generally produces more queries than any other area of the sport.

The transition from swimming to cycling is known as Transition 1 (T1). The transition from cycling to running is known as Transition 2 (T2). Each transition is very different. However, the main objective for both is to exit transition as quickly as possible.

The key to good transition is planning and preparation. By organising the right equipment in the right place you can make transition a much smoother process. Transition practice will allow you to familiarise yourself with the procedures of transition so that you will not be caught out on race day.

Triathlon makes great demands on the cardiovascular, muscular and central nervous systems. Each discipline uses different combinations of muscles, different intensities of loading, speeds of contraction and rhythm, and this can make shifting between disciplines very difficult if approached carelessly. This chapter contains information on how to improve your core strength to prevent this.

Transition 1

The major muscles needed in the swim are those in the upper body. The water supports bodyweight and upon exiting the water the body transfers from the horizontal to the vertical position and blood-supply demands change from the upper to the lower body quite rapidly; this can create a feeling of dizziness or disorientation particularly in novice athletes.

Triathletes leave the water and run into the transition area, which can be up to a few hundred feet away, or even more if the swim took place in an indoor pool. If the event comprises an *open water* swim, you

will be removing the wetsuit as you move, preparing either to unroll the vest or to bring the number belt from under the vest. The effort of these combined actions puts a great physical strain on the body, as oxygen demand is quite high. The body has to adapt to a full weight-bearing activity while moving very fast and performing complex motor skills. As you enter the transition area you should be virtually free of your wetsuit and your number should either be in place or should be ready to be put into place as soon as possible.

Upon arriving at the bike you will put on your helmet and sunglasses (if applicable, sunglasses should be placed inside the helmet ready) before touching the bike. You will then unrack the bike and proceed towards the transition exit and the mounting line. Upon reaching the mounting line, you will 'scoot' the bike along and then mount on the move before putting your feet into the shoes already attached to the pedals.

Transition 2

In cycling, the main muscles used are lower- and mid-body. The bike supports weight and in the bike-to-run transition the type of contraction in the quadriceps mean that two to three times the bodyweight is taken on each contact with the ground. Understanding this will help you to understand why it feels like you are running with somebody else's legs when you set out on to the run after the cycle section. It is vital that you get used to this feeling.

The bike-to-run transition should be very quick as you will loosen your shoes prior to arriving at the dismounting line. You will dismount on the move and then proceed towards your racking point. You rack your bike and remove your helmet and put on running shoes (preferably with lace lock system/elastic laces in place for speed), then proceed towards T2 exit to embark upon the run.

The adjustment between cycling and running is often very difficult because of the physiological changes outlined above. However, through practice this element of transition can be made much easier. One problem faced by novice and experienced triathletes alike is the issue of identifying their station. Care should be taken when setting up to help the athlete find their transition station in the heat of competition. Preparation is the key to a successful transition. The following checklists will help you:

Pre-race
- Check race gear;
- ensure running shoes have elastic laces and lace locks in place;
- secure number to vest or *race belt*.

Race day
- Arrive early;
- find racking stations and walk through transition identifying entry and exit points for T1 and T2;
- check the location of the mount/dismount line;
- prepare footwear, use talcum powder (see p. 114);
- ensure bike is in correct gear to start off;
- use Vaseline on cuffs/ankle/collar of wetsuit to aid removal and prevent chafing;
- ensure feeding bottles are prepared and put onto bike;
- rack bike;
- lay out equipment in logical order;
- get changed and go race!

GENERAL TRAINING FOR STRENGTH, POWER AND MUSCULAR ENDURANCE

If two athletes of the same weight are able to run the same distance at the same speed, they be said to be equally strong, i.e. they are able to apply the same force against the ground to propel them forward. However, if one of these athletes was to cover the distance in a shorter time, he could be said to be more powerful as a result of having performed the same work faster. If, however, these two individuals performed work at the same rate but one was able to keep going for twice the distance then he would be said to have greater muscular endurance.

Triathlon is a sport composed of cyclic skills, and these skills are usually endurance related. We could logically argue that triathlon is a sport where the dominant factor is muscular endurance, but nevertheless you should not overlook the contribution of power in this equation.

To develop power and muscular endurance to their optimum levels you must first develop a base level of strength, sometimes known as general strength. This can be viewed as the foundation for any future strength development. Neglecting or underdeveloping general strength can inhibit your eventual performance level.

Training for strength

Strength training is key to ensuring you remain injury free and able to utilise all of your hard training by giving you the strength to capitalise on your cardiovascular abilities. Strength training and conditioning is as important as the three disciplines and should be practised and trained as much as possible in the early and middle phases of training.

The goal of every athlete is to peak for his/her big race on the day, and the whole training schedule should be aimed at peaking for the most important competitions. Just as the swimming, cycling and running training should be arranged in this way so should strength training.

Earlier in this book I showed the principle of training using the overload and compensation model. This also applies to strength and conditioning training.

The aims and objectives of strength and conditioning training are listed below.

- **Develop ROM at the joints**: To achieve optimal muscular strength and therefore performance it is essential to exercise the joint through its full range of movement (ROM). A lack of flexibility around a joint or series of joints will prevent this and limit your potential. Additionally, lack of flexibility can also promote joint soreness and pain. Triathletes need good flexibility in all of the major joint areas and the development of this is a good starting point for any athlete who wants to engage in a strength-training programme.

- **Emphasise connective tissue strength**: Connective tissues are tendons and ligaments. Tendons attach muscles to bones and ligaments attach bones to other bones. In any training programme, muscles adapt much more quickly than tendons or ligaments. The temptation for any athlete is to progress the training schedule in line with the muscular response to activity, i.e. as muscle soreness reduces the training gets harder. The result of this is that the tendons and ligaments that will not have recovered as quickly are overused causing inflammation and soreness, which will have a negative impact on your training schedule. Adhering to this law requires the athlete to progress through the strength-training programme at a slow controlled rate allowing proper rest periods between gym sessions and unloading weeks every 14–21 days.
- **Start with the core and move out**: Strong core muscles (abdominals, lower back, hips) are essential to the work of the arms and legs. If the core muscles are weak then they provide a poor platform for the upper and lower limbs. Any long-term strength programme should attempt to develop core strength before that of the arms and legs.

- **Develop stabilisers before prime movers**: in the same way that the trunk muscles provide a strong platform for the arms and legs, well-conditioned stabilising muscles enable the prime movers to function more effectively. Stabilising muscles contract isometrically to fixate or immobilise a joint so that another joint can work. An example of this would be when shoulder is fixed allowing the elbow to flex and extend.
- **Train movements not muscles**: athletic performance is all about many muscle groups working together or in sequence. There are very few examples of muscle groups working in isolation although many training programmes include exercises where the trunk (for example) is in a fixed position. One of the principles stated earlier in this book was that of specificity. Applied in this context, athletes must aim to try and use exercises that closely mimic those found in the sport to optimise muscle development. There are times when you may need to ignore this particular guideline – during injury rehabilitation or when correcting a specific muscle imbalance problem, for example. At this point it may be necessary to attempt to isolate a muscle or group of muscles in the short term.

Developing core strength

A misguided yet popular philosophy for athletes persists: focus training on the region of the body most obviously needed to succeed in the sport.

Relating this misguided philosophy to the sport of triathlon would involve the athlete developing strength in the shoulders and upper back for swimming performance and the quadriceps, hamstrings gluteals and calves for cycling and running. The trunk region may receive some attention but this would probably be at the end of the programme as an afterthought. This is completely at odds with the principles raised earlier in this book

A more useful philosophy would be 'develop the core and move outwards', based on the fact that the core often initiates an action or enables movement transference from lower to upper body or vice versa. Hence the most important part of the body from an athlete's point of view should be the trunk region, which comprises abdominals, obliques, lower back and hip flexors.

Understanding the importance of the trunk musculature in athletic performance is one thing. You must also be able to condition the muscles to do their job effectively. Below are some examples of core conditioning programmes that you might use.

SAMPLE CORE CONDITIONING PROGRAMMES

	Phase 1	Phase 2	Phase 3	Phase 4
1	Swiss Ball hip extension shoulders on ball	SB hip extension/ flexion shoulders on ball	SB hip extension shoulders on ball – 1 leg balance	SB hip extension/ flexion shoulders on ball, 1 leg balance
	30–60 sec – 10 sec on 5 sec off	1 min - 3:3:3 tempo	1 min - 5 sec balances	1 min 3:3:3 tempo
2	Swiss Ball hip extension feet on ball	SB hip extension knee flexion	SB hip extension knee flexion one legged	SB hip extension knee flexion one legged – weighted
	30–60 sec – 10 sec on 5 sec off	1 min – 2:2:2 tempo	1 min – 2:2:2 tempo	1 min – 1:1:1 tempo
3	Squat and shoulder flexion – dumbbells	Squat and shoulder flexion – dumbbells	Overhead barbell squat	Overhead dumbbell squat
	30–60 sec	1 min	1 min	1 min
4	Swiss Ball back extension	SB back extension and shoulder flexion	SB back extension and shoulder flexion	SB back ext & shoulder flutter, scapula adduction & circles
	30–60 sec	1 min	1 min	1 min

5	Side lying glute leg raises	Side lying glute leg raises with external rotation	Standing glute med external rotations (against wall)	Standing glute med external rotations (against wall)
	30–60 sec	30–60 sec	1 min	1 min
6	One leg ¼ squat	One leg ½ squat	One leg squat on bench	One leg squat on bench, opp arm dumbell shoulder flexion
	30–60 sec	1 min	1 min	1 min
7	Arch walks and calf raise	Arch walks and calf raise	Arch walks and calf raise	Arch walks and calf raise
	30–60 sec	1 min	1 min	2 mins
8	Side planks, on knees	Side planks, on knees	Side planks, on feet	Side planks, on feet straight arms
	30–60 sec	1 min each side	1 min each side	1 min each side
9	Front planks, on knees	Front planks, on feet	Front planks, opposite arm and foot	Front planks, opposite arm and foot
	30–60 sec	30–60 sec	1 min	1 min
10	–	Step up – medicine ball overhead	Step up – barbell overhead	Step up – barbell overhead
		1 min	1 min	1 min
11	–	Split squat	Forward lunge	Forward & lateral lunge combination
		30 sec each leg	30 sec each leg	30 sec each leg
12	–	Horse stance vertical	Horse stance horizontal	Horse stance alphabet
		1 min	1 min	1 min

Developing stability

In any muscular action there are prime movers or agonists (those muscles which are directly involved in creating movement) and synergists (muscles that assist indirectly in the movement). For instance in a barbell curl the agonist is the biceps muscle and the synergists are the muscles surrounding the scapula (shoulder blade). Without this assistance the upper arm muscles would be less effective. The synergists limit unwanted movement, and are extremely important. If these stabilising muscles, which are often neglected in the conditioning process, are not strong enough to do their job properly then the prime movers have to try to do the work as well. This is in addition to their real objective. Ultimately, they end up doing neither task effectively with the result that you have too much unwanted movement and not enough power generated. This can cause strain and injury.

Problem areas for triathletes can include the pelvic area leading to hip and lower back pain, the shoulder girdle resulting in shoulder joint and neck pain and the lower leg.

Exercises to develop stabilising muscles often require only very light *resistance* as the muscle groups involved are relatively small. In many cases bodyweight will provide a sufficient resistance in the early stages of training. Other modes of resistance can include thera-bands and stretch cords, light dumbbells and small medicine balls.

Because the muscle groups in question will be called upon during general strength work they should be trained last in any programme or reserved for a separate training session altogether.

Performance enhancement training

This should form the initial phase of any conditioning programme and should be seen as the foundation for future strength work. In a 12-month programme this could generally be viewed as the reintroduction of resistance training after a period of active recovery.

The length of this phase depends upon experience and could be between 4–10 weeks.

One of the easiest ways to apply this type of work is through circuit training.

Circuit training

A sample circuit is shown overleaf. When you have read through this use the table below to construct your own circuit.

SAMPLE CIRCUIT	
Sample circuit using only bodyweight	**Sample circuit using bodyweight and dumbbells**
burpees	squat and overhead press
press ups	crunches
crunches	bent over rows
back extensions	lunges
lunges	back extensions
chin ups	press ups
squat thrusts	burpees
calf raise	triceps kickbacks
	kneeling torso rotations

When preparing a circuit workout, you should perform each exercise in turn moving down the programme in a vertical format.

- **Load**: bodyweight or a weight that can be used comfortably for the duration of the exercise.
- **Exercise per circuit**: 9–12 for novices, 6–9 for experienced athletes. Novices need to target as many muscle groups as possible.
- **Circuits per session:** novices, 2–3; experienced lifters, 3–5.
- **Rest between exercises**: 15–20 seconds (just enough time to move from station to station and weight selection).
- **Rest between circuits**: 1–3 minutes. Less experienced athletes will need a longer recovery time.
- **Frequency per week**: 2–4 depending upon experience. Regular lifters will recover more quickly regardless of the duration of this phase of training.

Maximal strength
It could be argued that a sport such as triathlon, where resistance to forward progress is minimal, does not require a high level of maximal strength.

There are, however, two arguments for the development of this component. Development of maximal strength to a certain level above that required during the event will result in the athlete having a greater strength reserve for any given action – fewer muscle fibres are recruited for the task, and so the action is performed far more efficiently.

The beauty of maximal strength training is that because it requires relatively heavy loads with low repetitions and medium to long rest periods the work leads primarily to activation of the central nervous system with the end result being an increase in strength with minimal hypertrophy (weight gain), as well as increased muscle co-ordination and synchronisation.

Power

The application of power during a triathlon of any distance is important. Often this is needed to overcome an increase in resistance such as a change of gradient or when slowing down for a turn and then regaining momentum. In many cases the power required will also involve endurance because one explosive effort will not be enough. When exiting a corner on the bike it might take 15–20 pedal strokes to get back up to pre-cornering speed (this obviously depends upon how much the athlete had to slow down). These strokes will generate much more force at a much higher rate than those required to maintain racing speed and therefore involve the fast-twitch fibres much more heavily.

Muscular endurance

Muscular endurance is the ability to apply force repeatedly without undue fatigue.

Events such as the triathlon require repeated muscular contraction over a long duration, so the dominant strength requirement is muscular endurance. To develop muscular endurance effectively requires a loading similar to that encountered in the activity with a high number of repetitions. In this and similar sports the athletes apply force against a standard resistance such as water, pedals or the ground over a very long duration. Energy for this activity comes predominantly from the aerobic system and so any strength training should be designed to enhance this.

You should take great care in choosing exercises that closely replicate movements found in the sport. The number of exercises and the work period for each should be chosen on the basis of the training status and tolerance level of each athlete.

As this type of work is closest to the intensity level of racing it makes up the final phase in race preparation. The duration of this cycle may last from 8 to 12 weeks

Some exercises you could use are shown overleaf.

SAMPLE EXERCISES FOR ENDURANCE TRAINING	
Exercise	**Specificity**
Step-up with knee drive	Applying force to the ground during running and practising the knee drive (i.e. as you push back up)
Straight leg deadlift	Hip extension in running or pedal stroke
Triceps kickback	Push part of front crawl stroke
Leg curls	pulling up on the pedal between 180° and 270° in the pedal cycle
Single leg press	Similar to act of pushing down on the pedal
Straight arm lat. pulldown	Similar to catch phase of front crawl stroke

An alternative proposition is to develop muscular endurance in a sport-specific manner. This could be achieved by the following.

SAMPLE ROUTINES TO DEVELOP MUSCULAR ENDURANCE	
Swim	Introduction of increased resistance such as drag shorts, hand paddles, pull buoy.
Bike	Riding in slightly bigger gear than normal so that rpm is reduced to 60–75 per min. Riding long hills.
Run	Running long hills.

Frequency of training

Training frequency refers to the number of training sessions undertaken in a set period of time. There are many variables that can affect this, some of which are only of relevance to elite lifters. The remainder may have some value when preparing your programme.

Training on three alternating days per week (say, Monday, Wednesday and Friday) is very effective as recovery time is important. Resistance training once every 10–14 days will be sufficient to maintain strength levels for many weeks

Most of the points made above are guidelines and should be treated as such. Use the principal of individuality when designing your own programme.

Overleaf is an example of a schedule that you might choose to use.

SAMPLE SCHEDULE

Exercise	Weeks 1–2	Weeks 3–4	Weeks 5–6	Weeks 7–8	Weeks 9–10
Lunges Straight arm lat. pulldown Triceps dips Single leg press Back extensions Crunches	Use 30% load and progressively perform 2 repetitions of work for each exercise	Perform the same work for 4 repetitions non-stop for each exercise	Perform the same work for 6 repetitions non-stop for each exercise	Perform 2 exercises non-stop or 12 repetitions of work Repeat for exercises 3 and 4 and exercises 5 and 6	Perform all 6 exercises for 36 repetitions non-stop
Rest between exercises	1–2 repetitions	2 repetitions	2 repetitions	2 repetitions	2 repetitions

LOAD ASSIGNMENT

When preparing a strength-training programme, a common stumbling block is the task of assigning a load for a particular exercise. How much should you lift for a given exercise? Is there a standard load based on age, gender or training status? You could take one of a number of approaches. If you are new to strength training or have only recently started lifting weights then any weight that is on the bar will provide an overload (see p. 30 for the concept of overload training). A more important goal in the first few weeks is to learn the correct technique and become comfortable with the whole process of weight training. In this instance your choice of load should be conservative for the first few sessions and, as you get to know your capacity, gradually raise the weight every two or three workouts. Within a few weeks you will be working to the required intensity for each set.

Load assessment should be undertaken in the following format:

- perform 10 repetitions with a relatively light weight (i.e. something you can lift without excessive force for 10 repetitions). Assess ease of completion;
- add more weight and perform 10 more repetitions;
- continue until 10 rm is reached (rm is the repetition maximum, meaning the maximum weight you can lift for 10 repetitions);
- allow rest of 2–4 min between trials.

Once the weight for a given rm is known then nominating the load to use in future workouts is a fairly simple process.

WEIGHT OF REPETITION MAXIMUM AS % OF 1 RM						
% of 1 rm	100	95	90	85	80	75
rm	1	2	4	6	8	10

PROGRAMME MAINTENANCE

One of the biggest mistakes you can make is to cease the strength and conditioning work just before or as the competitive phase begins. Many athletes believe, wrongly, that this type of training will detract from their competitive performances. In fact the opposite is true. There is no doubt that you should reduce your strength and conditioning work during the competitive phase but that doesn't mean it should be ignored. You can achieve this by following a pattern similar to the one shown below.

LEVEL OF S&C WORK DURING COMPETITIVE PHASE	S	M	T	W	T	F	S	S	M	T	W	T	F	S	S	M	T	W	T	F	S	S
Events 2 weeks apart	C			L	H				M	L			C									
Events 3 weeks apart	C			L	M				M	H	H					M	L					C

Where C = competition, L = low or light weight, M = moderate weight, H = hard or heavy weight.

In general the ideal maintenance programme should aim to use the minimum number of exercises to train the prime movers and an entire strength workout could be completed within 20–30 minutes with good planning. This would equate to 3–4 exercises with 2–4 sets per exercise. Care should be taken when planning in hip and leg exercises during this phase. If the athlete finds that this type of training fatigues the legs even more then they should be left out of the programme. At the very least core training and stability work should remain in the schedule.

06

NUTRITION

There are a myriad of books available at all levels on nutrition for health and sports performance. This book aims to look only at the direct requirements for training and racing over and above a good healthy diet.

CALORIFIC REQUIREMENTS

Triathlon is one of the toughest and most challenging sports in the world. The calorific requirement of any activity is directly related to the level of intensity coupled with the duration of effort. When looking at the calorific burn of any activity you must focus on the additional calories used over and above what would have been used if you'd stayed at home watching the television or sitting at your office desk. The average female burns around 2000 calories per day and the average male around 2400 calories, which broadly speaking translates into 150–200 calories per hour while awake.

Running at a moderately hard pace might burn off an additional 400–500 calories (1600–2000 kilojoules) per hour, although most running sessions would last an hour or less in duration. Cycling at a similar perceived effort, because you are seated and weight supported, might only use 300 or so extra calories per hour but you are likely to be able to continue at that pace for 2 hours or more. Of course, because of the gears and the fact you can freewheel downhill it is easy to cycle at a much lower effort or intensity that you can run at, so a 3-hour really slow bike ride might actually burn fewer calories than a 45-minute hard fast run. To increase your calorie-burn when cycling, rides must be moderately hard and around 90 minutes to 2 hours in duration.

FAT BURNING

One of the biggest misconceptions in training and weight management is the concept of long slow exercise sessions being good for 'fat burning'. If this were true then elite racing cyclists would all be on the podgy side and far-travelling cyclo-tourists all mega-skinny. There is quite obviously something flawed in this argument!

Certainly the fuel for long steady miles will come largely from the metabolism of fat. However, as mentioned above the rate of calorie burn is quite slow and it is easy to take on board more calories in the form of snacks and energy bars at a faster rate than you are using them on this type of ride.

Faster and harder training at a manageable but moderate effort work rate will increase the total number of calories burned. Although a lower percentage may come from fat the fact that the total number is greater means that you actually end up burning more fat calories by riding at this brisker pace.

Short, hard racing or training efforts are fuelled almost entirely from carbohydrate and protein-derived calories. However, this sort of riding has a high calorific burn rate and increases your metabolic rate. This in turn means that, by the end of the day, you'll have used up a significant total number of calories of which a good percentage will have come from fat metabolism while recovering from the training.

The table below summarises three different types of training and how they fit into a race-training and weight-control plan.

TRAINING TYPE BENEFITS

Training type	Training benefit	Weight-control benefit
Long steady sessions, riding 2 or more hours at the sort of pace you can easily hold a conversation at.	Hours spent in activity strengthen supporting muscles, and improve all-round blood flow and stamina	Fairly low calorie burn per hour but makes up for it in the total number of hours of training that can be achieved – just be careful you don't put all the calories back in at the café stop though.
Moderate intensity – moderate duration riding, running, swimming; typically 60–90-min riding time, shorter in swim and run.	Maximum training benefits in terms of aerobic fitness and endurance. The ability to work at a good rate of effort for a sustained period.	Fairly high calorie-burn including fat calories. Best training mode for weight loss as can be sustained for reasonable time period.
Fast, short, intense and hard training.	Race specific speed and strength, improves top end power and climbing abilities.	High calorific burn plus changes to muscles increase resting metabolic rate and so day-to-day calorie burn, in short, the reason elite athletes are so lean.

Turbo training at a moderate to high intensity improves fitness and burns calories

FUELLING TRAINING

In order to fuel your training you must ensure that you are getting the right type of fuel into your body at the right time. Just like a car the body must have fuel in the system for it to perform. Training without fuel in the system is at best going to have limited benefit and at worse could cause serious problems.

The best approach is to ensure that there is sufficient fuel in the system before you set off on your training session or race. Different people seem to be able to train hard after very differing timeframes post-eating. This will also depend on what you have eaten. Typically, easier to digest foods can be eaten closer to the training time and the easier the training session the closer to it you can eat.

For a race event or high-intensity session you might only be able to tolerate having eaten 2 hours before riding but for a steady miles session a light snack before you leave might be OK.

Putting the fuel in before you train not only makes for fuelling the training effort but also in terms of weight control you put the additional calories in and burn them off leaving few excess calories in the system.

Early morning training or race events are the hardest to cater for. Practise your chosen regime in training so that you know what works best for you before your first race. A bowl of cereal with a whey-protein-based supplement, a low-fat cheese-spread sandwich or a bowl of low-fat rice pudding along with plenty of water or dilute energy drink taken about 60–90 minutes before the session

(maybe 2 hours before for a hard race) works well for most people. Although brown bread and wholegrain cereals may be better for overall nutrition, for a pre-training meal you want something easy and quick to digest so opt for white bread, white rice and the like and save your wholegrains for non-training days.

Do try to ensure that you include protein such as a portion of meat or fish in your pre-training meal as it is important for fuelling performance as well as in the post-training recovery and muscle adaptation. Try to keep the fat content down as it will slow down the digestion process.

Training in the evening after work can also present problems. One sensible option is to have a double-lunch! Eating your lunch a little earlier than usual followed by a mid-afternoon snack will mean you aren't training on an empty stomach and won't need such a big meal after training and before bed. Furthermore by moving some of the evening calories to earlier in the day you are putting the calories into training rather than your waistline.

Suitable foods for your mid-afternoon snack might be a tuna and pasta salad, rice salad, a lean meat sandwich or a jacket potato. You might also consider having an energy drink with your snack to ensure a good mix of carbohydrates along with the protein and fat of the snack. Cereal bars or special energy bars work well too but do check the fat content isn't too high.

After training you will need to refuel and rehydrate. How much you need to take on board in terms of calories will depend on whether or not you are trying to lose excess weight and when your next training ride or race is. Many of the sport science training manuals refer to a magic window some 20–60 minutes after exercise when the systems of the body are at their optimum for refuelling. While it is very important to ensure that you replenish spent energy supplies as soon as possible after exercise if you are in a stage race or on a training camp where you are riding day after day at a hard level, for the majority of riders a more gradual approach to refuelling may be better. After all if, for example, you have done a 2-hour endurance ride on a Sunday morning with Monday typically being a rest day, the next time you train might well be Tuesday evening. Under those circumstances a normal, well-balanced diet will suffice to ensure the energy stores are replenished without risking additional surplus calories.

If you are due to train or race the next day then you must replace the spent calories and top up your energy reserves. The best way to do this is by having a simple carbohydrate, energy-rich snack or drink as soon as possible after your ride. Recovery drinks and bars are ideal but any wholesome low-fat cereal bar will be almost as good. You also need to ensure you rehydrate fully so take on board plenty of water or dilute energy drink.

If you are trying to lose some weight and aren't due for a hard session the next day, then a light protein-rich snack such as a chicken or tuna salad should be sufficient. If, however, you find yourself feeling light headed then remember to take in some extra calories.

SPORTS DRINKS AND HYDRATION

Having the correct fuel in the body is important but even more critical is ensuring that you keep yourself hydrated. This applies not only to during training and racing but also before and after riding.

Just a 1 per cent reduction in hydration levels can result in a 10 per cent reduction in performance and a loss of 25 per cent or more fluid can have serious medical consequences.

For short training sessions of 45 minutes or less plain water will be fine – around 500 ml per hour in cool weather and up to a litre on very hot days. However, by virtue of complex molecular science, water is absorbed more quickly into the body if the drink contains a small amount of salts and sugars. Such drinks are referred to as 'hypotonic', electrolyte or rehydration formulas and are ideal for short summer rides or if you are prone to profuse sweating.

Remember though, that the salts and sugars in these drinks are at a very low level and are there to promote hydration. They are not there in high enough amounts to provide energy. You can cheaply and easily make your own hypotonic hydration drink by mixing about 20 ml of fresh orange juice into a 750-ml bottle of water and adding a very small pinch of table salt.

For energy replacement you need what is referred to as an 'isotonic' drink (as opposed to 'hypotonic', which is solely for mineral salt replacement). Some formulas will do both but read the labels. Energy drink formulas contain what are known as complex or long chain carbohydrates, which break down at a steady rate releasing energy into the bloodstream at a controlled rate. They don't simply provide a burst of sugar but offer a more sustained energy supply. Electrolyte formulas aid hydration with the added bonus of replacing salts lost through sweat and thereby reducing the risk of cramps and muscle spasms.

As isotonic drinks provide a steady supply of fuel rather than a single shot you should start using them early on in a training session. If your training session is going to be over 60 minutes long, or you weren't able to eat much in the hours leading up to training, then these drinks will be a big bonus. Aim to drink one 500-ml bottle per hour – topping up to 750 ml per hour by adding extra water if it's hot or if you tend to sweat a lot. This will both aid energy supply and prevent dehydration.

The further you are into your training sessions the more important the hydration element is as, hopefully, you'll have kept your energy stores topped up so far. For this reason on a typical 2-hour summer endurance training session one bottle of energy formula and one bottle of hydration/electrolyte formula will be ideal. In the winter two energy formula bottles might be more appropriate.

For a short, hard training session or short race of less than an hour, assuming you topped up your energy stores previously, one bottle of the energy drink will be fine. Then, on returning home drink a bottle of the rehydration/electrolyte formula – or your home-made mix – to aid muscle recovery. Some proprietary recovery formula drinks also contain protein, which can also aid recovery especially after long or hard training sessions.

For long steady training sessions alternate energy and hydration remembering that energy is more important in the first half of the training sessions and hydration in the second.

So in summary, you need to ensure that you are well hydrated and your energy tanks are full prior to training and racing. You need to balance your calorific intake with the duration and intensity of your training. A good healthy and balanced diet with plenty of carbohydrate and lean protein along with a healthy level of fat intake will ensure that your body can refuel between exercise sessions.

AFTER THE RACE

After successfully completing your first race you will hopefully want to go on and do more events. After the race you need to give your body a week to recover and then maybe pick the training plan up again from Phase 2 this time with just two weeks of race endurance training and then two weeks from Phase 3 as speed training.

After these four weeks of training another *taper week* can take you to your second key race. In the meantime training races and club time-trials can still form part of your race training but, at least in the first instance, try not to target more than one race per month. This should allow you to improve your base fitness as well as race specific training.

Ideally you should include some Phase 1-type training not just at the start of your race career but every month or so after that with a longer period of base training during the winter. Remember the analogy that you need a strong foundation to build a tall structure and the peak can only be as high as the base will support. You might also decide to enlist a coach to help you plan your training and your racing and focus on specific goals and targets.

INJURY AND ILLNESS

When considering injury prevention we need to look at the ways in which you may sustain injury:

1. Injuries relating from contact with the ground.
2. Injuries resulting from contact with other participants.
3. Injuries resulting from poor technique.
4. Injuries resulting from unsuitable equipment.
5. Injuries resulting from unsuitable clothing and footwear.
6. Injuries resulting from inappropriate training programmes.
7. Injuries caused by lack of fitness or sudden increase in volume of training.
8. Injuries resulting from inappropriate training loads.

9. Injuries exacerbated by lack of treatment.
10. Injuries that reoccur through insufficient recovery.

Most of these types of injury can be prevented by being careful and planning what you are doing. Injury types 1 and 2 are generally the result of trips and falls and while nobody plans to fall, by being careful about the surface you run and ride on you can reduce the risk considerably. Injury types 3, 4, 5 and 6 are all related and by following the guidelines in this book you will avoid picking up this kind of injury. Injury types 7 and 8 can be avoided by following the planning and training guidelines we have established and by being careful when coming back from illness. The approach to returning to training after illness is very similar to the approach to returning after injury outlined below.

Recovering from injury and illness

When an injury occurs it is often tempting to continue to train through it ignore the pain and hope it will go away. It won't. If you suffer from a twist or fall then apply the RICE principle:

- Rest
- Ice
- Compression
- Elevation.

If this does not have an effect on reducing pain and swelling then you should seek medical advice as soon as possible. This could take the form of a GP or hospital visit. Depending on the outcome you should then seek out some form of remedial therapy. There are many sports therapists practising in the UK, however, many of them have only basic qualifications and differing degrees of training. As with most things local recommendations are the best and approaching a local triathlon or single discipline club will be the best way to find a suitable practitioner. GPs have differing approaches to sport and some will simply say don't take part at all while others may be more sympathetic and more constructive with their advice. Follow any guidelines issued by therapist or doctors and do not rush back to training as this could cause a more serious issue and a much longer break from training. Work around the injury – for example if the injury is running or cycling related then focus on swimming and core stability and strength and conditioning work. This is a great way to keep going and is one of the real benefits of triathlon. Indeed, it is often the reason people get involved in triathlon in the first place.

When approaching training after an injury, do not be tempted to rush back in – you will need to build up slowly on the recovering area. You will not be able to instantly return to your previous volume and intensity on the recovering area

and you will need to carefully build back up over a number of weeks. Don't rush, don't take short cuts and don't ignore any symptoms or problems that you may not have recovered from properly.

FURTHER DEVELOPMENT

If you have just completed your race you may be feeling a little lost. Your motivation for training may be sliding and you are not sure what to do next. Regardless of whether you have completed a sprint event with a target of completion or an ironman event with a specific target for completing in a given time you will know whether or not you achieved your target. If you did, then well done! If you didn't, then it is important to establish what stopped you. Pause and review so you can prevent the specific circumstance arising again.

Now is the time to pick your next target event, but don't be tempted to make it too soon as you need at least a few weeks to recover and then a few more weeks to get back into preparation. If you do want to have another attempt in the same racing season this may be perfectly possible depending on the race distance. A sprint event will require less

recovery and less preparation than an ironman event with standard- and middle-distance somewhere between the two. It is not possible or advisable to attempt a subsequent ironman or middle-distance race in the same season but a sprint or standard-distance race may be possible providing you have enough of a break.

If your target was to achieve a specific time and you missed this, consider how much you missed it by and look at the time splits provided by the race organiser. You will usually be given time splits for swimming, cycling and running, and many races can now tell you how long you spent on each transition. This can be very useful as it will allow you to see where your weaknesses were. At this point you will probably also need to consider whether your targets were really achievable specific to the course you raced on. A target time based on a flat run and bike course will be drastically increased by the course having hills

and undulations in it. This may be a factor and comparing the winning times with those on a flatter course will give you an idea of the extra time the race takes in these conditions. When reviewing your performance always look for the positives and build on these while developing your weaknesses. Once you have identified which areas need work, you can revisit the planning chapter and start to plan for another event.

You may have had a great race and achieved or exceeded your expectations, in which case what now? Do you want to race faster and/or longer? If you are moving up in distance then increasing your training by 10 per cent per week will give you a really good basis for the planning required once you have identified an event. This method can be used over any distance and is a good, safe way of increasing training and developing athletes. If you want to go faster then using the interval method described in the discipline-specific chapters will get you moving in the right direction and using your split times from the race will help to show you where there is room for improvement. Being very analytical about every aspect of your performance in the race will also help you target areas of improvement either in terms of fitness or technique. Looking at everything from swim starts, pack swimming, turning, transition running from swim, transition to bike, bike technique and handling, as well as the psychological effects of racing will give you clear indications of where you need to focus your attention for improvement.

Joining a club

Now would also be a great time to get involved with a club if you have not already done so. There are over 350 triathlon clubs in the UK and there are many more discipline-specific clubs so you are sure to find a club of some description near you that will be able to help you. This will add an additional aspect to your training and help keep you motivated at times when you may need some extra lift.

MAINTENANCE PROGRAMMES

If you simply want to maintain the fitness you have worked so hard to achieve then you need to plan a maintenance programme. This is much easier than planning your training programme as it is simply a case of using the time planner (see Appendix) to outline a manageable and long-term set of training slots over a given period. Once you have done this you can see where your sessions will be and you can then allocate disciplines to the sessions. The good news is that once you have achieved a level of fitness and worked really hard to get there you do not need to work anything like as hard to maintain it and, provided you keep up the intensity, you can drastically reduce the volume, duration and frequency of training. If you are a long-distance triathlete then you may find your endurance suffers with fewer long-distance sessions, but this will come back quite quickly should you want to go back to racing.

Finally as you are now an athlete and an experienced triathlete keep progressing on that road. Triathlon is a unique sport and you can be a European or world champion in many age categories and over a variety of distances so the sky really is the limit.

APPENDIX: PLANNING FORMS

Our first planning form (overleaf) is designed to enable you to work out what time you have to fit in training with the rest of your life commitments. This is really important to ensure you identify the opportunities that you do have to train as well as ensuring that you have sufficient time for work, family, rest and other play.

(These forms can be downloaded from www.bloomsbury.com/uk/triathlon-the-go-faster-guide-9781408832271.)

PLANNING FORM – FITTING IN YOUR WEEKLY TRAINING

	Monday	Tuesday	Wednesday	
05.00 a.m.				
05.30				
06.00				
06.30				
07.00				
07.30				
08.00				
08.30				
09.00				
09.30				
10.00				
10.30				
11.00				
11.30				
Noon				
12.30 p.m.				
1.00				
1.30				
2.00				
2.30				
3.00				
3.30				
4.00				
4.30				
5.00				
5.30				
6.00				
6.30				
7.00				
7.30				
8.00				
8.30				
9.00				
9.30				
10.00				

	Thursday	Friday	Saturday	Sunday

This planner is to help you work out the long-term planning. You can use this for number of sessions in each discipline. Or you can use it to write your goals; either way you should use it for a long-term view of where you are heading to.

PLANNING FORM – LONG-TERM AND CROSS-DISCIPLINE			
Week	Swim	Bike	Run
1			
2			
3			
4			
5			
6			
7			
8			
9			
10			
11			
12			
13			
14			
15			
16			
17			
18			
19			
20			
21			
22			
23			
24			
25			
26			

This is the 'your week at a glance' form. It enables you to plan a week's training in advance built around what the more detailed planner above tells you.

PLANNING FORM – YOUR WEEK AT A GLANCE				
	Swim	Bike	Run	Transition	Other
Mon					
Tue					
Wed					
Thu					
Fri					
Sat					
Sun					

This is the session planner, and will be needed for each session that you do. The more detail that you record the more useful this form will be.

PLANNING FORM – SESSION PLAN			
Day		Discipline	
Time		Location	
Warm-up			
Main body			
Cool down			
Stretching			
Comment			

GLOSSARY

Aerobic fitness: The ability of an individual to undertake activity while using oxygen as a fuel.

Anaerobic: The ability of an individual to undertake intensive activity at a level at which the body is no longer using oxygen as a fuel.

Aquathlon: An event comprising a swim followed directly by a run.

Best pace: The fastest speed you can sustain for the distance covered. Knowing and applying the principle of best pace is essential to becoming a successful triathlete.

Bottom bracket: The section at the bottom of the bicycle where the chainring and cranks are joined through the frame. A point that requires great rigidity.

Cadence: The speed at which you complete a given action. It is most commonly used in cycling to refer to the number of times you revolve the pedals in one minute (expressed as revolutions per minute, or rpm). It can also be used in swimming and running to refer to the number of strokes you perform or the number of times your foot hits the floor in a minute.

Catch point: After your arm enters the water, it will travel a short distance under the water before your hand 'catches' and you start to feel the resistance of the water, before you pull against it moving your hand and arm under your head and body. Do not start the pulling action too soon, but press with your fingers and keep your wrist firm.

Chainring: The large sprocket attached to the pedals in the centre of the bike. Usually there will be two or possibly three chainrings attached to the pedals by cranks.

Clipless pedals: Pedals that attach to the bottom of the shoes usually using a mechanism of springs.

Conditioning: The physical state of readiness for any given individual.

Drafting: The practice of gaining an advantage by racing behind somebody else. Most effective in cycling and within 5 m of the rider in front though there is also a benefit in the swim and run. There are rules preventing this in the majority of triathlon. See also non-drafting.

Draft-legal racing: A draft-legal race is one where athletes are allowed to ride close to one another, benefiting from the 'drafting' effect of being in another cyclist's slipstream.

Drills: The practice of repeating a small portion of a skill often in an exaggerated form to enhance the ability of an athlete in performing the skill in race conditions.

Duathlon: An event comprising a run followed directly by a cycle followed by a final run.

Endurance: The ability to sustain a given workload for a long period.

Fartlek: From the Swedish for 'speed play', this is a training method that combines continuous training with interval training.

Flexibility: The ability of an athlete to move a limb around the joint in the full range of movement.

Gears: The collection of sprockets that are used on bicycles to vary the resistance and speed of progress. There will be a gear mechanism at the back and probably also at the front near the chainring.

Headset: The section where handlebars and stem meet the frame of your bicycle and swivel.

Hydration: The liquids you drink. A well-hydrated individual would have consumed sufficient appropriate liquids to sustain life and activity at an optimum level.

Intensity: The level at which you undertake a given action or exercise is referred to as the intensity. Working very hard would be an intensive workout, while working out very gently would be a low-intensity workout.

Interval training: The practice of using small intervals of time within a training session where the training is extremely hard. This is to replicate the demands of racing in small chunks to help the athlete improve.

Ironman: A long-distance race of a 2.4-mile ocean swim, 112-mile bike race and 26.2-mile run; also a registered trade name.

Lactate threshold: The highest intensity at which the body can function before the production of lactic acid exceeds the ability of the body to reprocess it.

Lactic acid: The waste product from the muscles when the body operates anaerobically.

National governing body: Each sport has a body which represents the interests of that sport in that country. Within Britain it is the British Triathlon Association and above this there is the European and international triathlon unions. To compete at national championship level or above you must be a member of your national governing body.

Non-drafting: An event where drafting is not allowed.

Open water: A piece of water such as a lake, reservoir, sea or river that is used for swimming. An outdoor pool would not be considered to be open water.

Power meter: A device that you can buy to fit to your bike, which will measure your power output when pedalling and display the results (for example your maximum power, your immediate power on starting to pedal and your average power throughout the session) on a screen mounted on your handlebars.

Race belt: A belt worn with the sole purpose of displaying a race number so that it can be moved from the front during a run and to the back during the cycle section.

Resistance training: This is developing strength by making your muscles react against a resisiting force, for example, pushing, pulling or squeezing. Therabands and stretch cords are useful for this kind of training.

Saddle height: The height measured from the top of the pedal axles to the top of the saddle. Not to be confused with frame height.

Sprint: A flat out effort at top speed.

Sprint distance: A race that is much shorter in distance. Strictly speaking it is a race of half the distance of the standard distance but often the distances are much shorter.

Standard distance: Often referred to as Olympic distance as it is this race distance that is competed over in the Olympic games. The race is 1500 m swim, 40 km bike and 10 km run.

Static trainer: Often referred to as a turbo trainer. Normally an A-frame that holds the back wheel of a bicycle while applying a roller to the back wheel of the bicycle for resistance.

Strength: Can describe either maximal strength, which is the ability of an individual to complete a given workload in very short amounts, for example lifting a very large weight once; or muscular strength and endurance, which is the ability of an individual to sustain a workload for an extended period.

Taper week: This is where you reduce the intensity of training in the week prior to your event.

Transition: The area in triathlon where your equipment will be stored and you will enter.

Turbo trainer: Also known as a 'static trainer', this is a piece of equipment, generally an A-frame, that holds the back wheel on a small roller to allow the rider to pedal against resistance for training purposes. Early models simply used fans to provide resistance, hence the name 'turbo trainer', but more up-to-date models use internal fluid or magnets to provide the training resistance required. While they have improved in recent years, turbo trainers still make a lot of noise and take up a lot of space.

Trisuit: A specially made suit of one or two pieces and used for the duration of a triathlon.

VO$_2$max: This is the maximum amount of oxygen an individual can use during exercise. Normally expressed as litres of oxygen used per minute (l/min), or relative to the athlete's size in millilitres per kilo per minute ml/kg/min.

Wetsuit: A suit used for swimming made from neoprene. The suit is designed to trap a layer of water between the body and the suit which is then warmed by the body.

INDEX